MAILING LISTS UNBOXED

The Three-year, No-bestseller Plan For Making A Sustainable Living From Your Fiction Book 2

PATTY JANSEN

Get FREE ebooks

Visit pattyjansen.com
to sign up for Patty's mailing list. You get four series starter ebooks for free!

ONE

This Is A Book About Email Marketing For Authors

I HEAR IT ON PODCASTS, on forums, everywhere I turn. Self-published writers ask the same old question: how can I keep my books selling?

Invariably, they are advised to run a few ads, to lower their price, to run Facebook ads, or to do a cross-promotion—all valid techniques.

But none, absolutely *none* of them mention the most powerful way to keep your backlist selling: your author mailing list.

Oh, many authors *have* a mailing list, and talk about gaining subscribers, but once people are on that list, the authors are not quite sure what to do with them.

Is it because authors are shy?

Because they're afraid to bother people?

Because they're afraid to sound like a salesperson?

Or they're just afraid they'll happen to annoy someone?

I don't know, but many authors are sitting on this bunch of

potential in the form of a few thousand email addresses—and they're doing next to nothing with it.

They complain that their books aren't selling in between releases, and that they need to fight for sales, *while doing nothing with the people who have already shown themselves to be interested in their books*, or at least have shown themselves willing to receive emails from those authors.

I know, it's nuts.

So in this book I'll be doing something about that.

This is not a book for beginners without a list. If you want to know the principles of a mailing list and how to set one up, I have described the basic processes in *Self-publishing Unboxed*. In that book, a 101 guide to self-publishing, I described what you need in order to run an author mailing list, I've discussed websites, landing pages, companies to use and things to look out for. If you don't have a list yet and want to know what you need, go and read that book first. That's what it's for.

In this book we go into much more detail about what you can actually *do* with your mailing list once you have all these things set up.

This particular book, and the entire concept of the *Three-year, No-bestseller Plan For Making A Living From Your Fiction*, was born from my belief that authors are not using their mailing lists to their full potential. A mailing list is not just a service of the author to their reader, it is also an extremely powerful marketing tool.

This book will show you basic principles of different types of mailing lists, how to use your list to engage your readers, how to set up your list to perform basic automated tasks that help you sell your books, and how to set it up so that you will never have to buy an ad on another listing service again.[1]

Who am I to write this book? As I said in *Self-publishing Unboxed*, I used mailing lists back in the early 2000's when I didn't understand anything about mailing lists or know why they were working so well. Back then, there were no services to handle mass email ("mass" meaning more than 20 emails, LOL), and there were no services to deal with any of the things that we now consider standard, including spam blocking. There was a lot of spam, and it all went into your inbox, especially if you owned a domain.

Anyway, back in those days, I sold non-fiction print books. They were specialist books that were often rare and never cheap. I would sometimes buy libraries from estates of the deceased, make a list and email it out to the 150-odd people on my mailing list. Yes, the only way you could do this was by copying their addresses in the Bcc field! And by doing this, I noticed the efficiency of marketing through lists. No ads to buy, no stuff to photocopy and staple, no folders to mail. It was a huge saving especially in terms of time. And it was much easier to reach people.

Fast forward to the present, and I'm writing fiction. I self-published my first book after selling some stories and books with traditional publishers. But unlike selling physical books—where you always get the buyer's address, because otherwise how can you send the book?—with ebooks you have no idea who your buyers are. Amazon does. Apple does. Kobo does. So when your book is delivered to the buyer, you can't slip in a flyer for something else that you think might interest the buyer. This had been a major source of sales for me. I would colour code the paper of the flyers so I knew where it came from if someone mailed me (you remember mail and postage stamps?) an order. You can't do that with ebooks delivered by a third party.

I was not used to that, and didn't like that situation at all, so when people started talking about mailing lists, I jumped on the bandwagon. Over the past few years, I have made a liveable income doing this.

TWO

Why You Might Not Like To Read This Book

THIS BOOK IS NOT GOING to be for everyone.

This book is about mindset and strategy. It's not about paint-the-dots examples. This book is designed to make you think, not to tell you what to do. This book also assumes that, armed with the ideas you will get and your wits, you'll be able to read the help files of your mailing list provider (or, for that matter, Google) to check on how exactly to set things up in your particular mailing list provider. Each of them (MailerLite, MailChimp, AWeber, ConvertKit) treats lists and subscribers in such a different manner that it would be impossible for me to give a single step-by-step how-to in this book. Besides, I don't want to. It's boring stuff, and seriously, you can read, so check the help files. That's what they're for, and they're always the most recent and up-to-date source of information.

Also, I would say that you need an open mind to dive into the possibilities of what you can do with your list.

But it could be that you have already decided that you only want to use your list to talk to your existing fans about snippets of new books and your cats.

That's OK. It's a valid use of a newsletter and I like cats. But in this case, if you have made such a clear decision about how to use your list already, then you may not get a lot out of this book, because this book is for people who want to use the full potential of mailing lists. A chatty newsletter to your readers is just one very small part of how you can use it. Not that you *shouldn't* use it like that, not at all. I do. Except I don't have cats.

But you can do so much more with your list. So even if you're such a writer and you're curious, or you're wondering if you're somehow missing out on something good, then read on.

Especially if you're a writer who fears "bothering people" by sending email to the subscribers on their list.

Because you know those preconceptions you have about who is on that list and why? They're mostly wrong.

THREE

Leave Your Preconceptions At The Door

COME IN, COME IN. The door is open and everyone is welcome here.

There is a little table next to the door, where you can leave your preconceptions, your *assumptions*, your *opinions* about mailing lists. You can deposit your opinions on landing pages there, as well, and automated emails and—gasp—popup forms, too.

It's OK, no one will touch them while you read, and they'll still be there once you finish reading. Warning: I'd hazard a guess that you may not want some of them back. For that purpose, there is also a bin next to the table.

This book operates under only one principle, which I feel you should apply to your whole career:

If it doesn't take a huge amount of money or time, try it. If it works, do more of it.

Don't ask fellow authors if you should do something. If you ask fellow authors, you will find that there is no shortage of assumptions and opinions when it comes to mailing lists, processes to recruit people and what to do when those people are on that list. Most of those opinions are negative. Most of them are self-destructive.

You know the schtick:

- "I hate popups!"
- "I never subscribe to mailing lists!"
- "They just send me spam!"
- "As soon as a site asks me to sign up, I leave and never come back!"
- "People who subscribe are just after freebies!"

And so on, and so forth.

For the most part, those opinions and preconceptions get in your way. Why? Because the preconceptions may only apply to a small percentage of people, vocal though they are. Because you believe that these people do as they say.

For example the people who say that they'll never come back if a site has a popup that asks them to sign up. Do you think they *really* follow through with this? Well, if they did, most of the Internet would be off-limits to them. And just think about all the energy they would need to spend trying to remember which sites ask for sign-ups. They might even need to keep a *list* of these sites.

Of course these people don't follow through with their statement. Not only that, but when they want to get something, they'll sign up. They'll complain to high heaven, but they'll sign up. It is not about these people. At least, it's not about them as individuals.

Your task is to figure out, through testing, which method gives you the best results for the aim you have set. Determine which result you want, try it, and see what happens. Use a pop-up sign-up form on you website for a set period, and don't use one for another period. Check how many sign-ups you get for each 100 unique visits for each period. Make your decision based on this, not on the comments of a few.

So here is lesson one: It's not about what people *say*, it's about what people *do*.

The above just concerns the preconceptions of other people. Never mind the most damaging preconceptions of all: your own.

You don't want to do something because *you* would never be swayed by a certain tactic. You don't want to do something because you don't like this thing.

As an individual, you are but a grain of sand in the avalanche of humanity. Don't get me wrong: so am I, and so is everyone else. But in your mind, you, and your way of thinking, are majority speak. For successful marketing, this mindset gets in your way. You may indeed be part of a majority opinion. Most likely, you are not. At any rate, you can't assume that you are or aren't for your particular audience.

So what can you do?

You test it on your audience. You evaluate the results. Don't let yourself be led by a few loudmouths who don't do as they say, or by your own preconceptions.

Oh, while you're at it and you're still in the hall, put your sense of wanting to be liked by everyone in this little box here. Yes, it's called a *safe* and I'll throw the key into a deep and cold pond. I'll give you a net at the end of the book, but you probably won't need it.

Go forth, step into the inner sanctum, and be preconception-free.

FOUR

Repeating The Three-Year Plan

NOW THAT WE got that out of the way, I'd like you to read the original text of the Three-Year Plan again. In *Self-publishing Unboxed*, we have visited the areas that need to be set up: the quality of the book, the cover, the description, the branding of the series, your website and how to set up your mailing list. Now read it again, taking note of the points lower down in the plan.

The Three-Year, No-bestseller Plan To Making A Sustainable Income From Your Writing

I. The Product

1. Write a series of three books in a genre you like. It's best if the books are full-length of 70-80k words at least. There are people who can get away with novellas, but selling well gets harder the shorter your books are. Unless, maybe, your genre is erotica or romance. Maybe. Just make the books full length, OK? It makes life so much easier (insert whisper that

sounds like Bookbub: many advertising sites don't accept short books).
2. Make the first book free.
3. Play around a bit with advertising if you feel so inclined (I mean—why the hell not?), but don't worry about stuff that takes you away from writing too much.
4. Make sure you have the following in all your books: a link to your mailing list sign-up form, and, at the end, a live link to the next book in the series.
5. When you finish the series, or even while you're writing it, start the next series. Make it a slightly different subgenre, or use a different setting and characters. Make sure that people don't need to have read the other series in order to follow it. Write three books. Make the first book free.
6. Repeat 5. Twice, if you can. Three years @ 4 novels a year = 12 books = 4 trilogies.
7. Advertise your freebies, but don't fall down any rabbit holes that take you away from writing for major chunks of time (insert snort that sounds like Facebook advertising).

II. The Marketing

1. After a while, your mailing list will start to build up a bit (see point 4 above). Get a paid account at MailChimp or wherever you are. If you are not at a list provider that allows automation and segmentation, and most importantly, automation *based on* automatic segmentation, move your list.
2. Set up mailing automation. When people join your list, send them an email with the freebies, even though they're already free. Don't email the freebies to them, but include download links in the email.

Then booby-trap those links so that you can track who downloads what. You'll be using this later.
3. Next, send your subscribers to an automated program that sends them something at regular intervals (Amazon genre newsletters arrive every two weeks, that's good enough for me). What do you write about? About you, about your fiction, free short stories, you ask them questions, tell them about tidbits of research you've done, or places you travelled for your writing. Tell them about box sets you're in, and even plug your friends with similar books. Anything. Booby-trap any links to your books so your MailChimp/AWeber/whatever account knows who clicked what.
4. Siphon people who clicked all the links to series 1 (and downloaded the freebie!) off to a side list, and say three months later send them an email saying: hey, this is book 2 in the series. Do this with all books 2 in all your series.
5. Repeat steps 3 and 4. Create new emails, use the links and who clicks them to segment your list and send them further information based on who clicked what.
6. Pronto! You have now created your own marketing machine that crawls like a giant slug over your subscriber list.

III. Your Tasks

It's now really clear what you need to do:

1. Keep writing new books that people want to read, continuing your most popular series, starting new series maybe (make book 1 free again). Add new emails about those books to your mailing sequence.
2. Keep feeding people into your giant mailing slug.

The things we dealt with in *Self-publishing Unboxed* were all extremely important to get right before you do anything else. In fact, they are the foundation of the plan. Everyone knows that without foundations, you have a lousy building. Without at least one series with multiple books, and a decent sell-through, none of this will work. If you don't have this, if your sell-through is not good, if you have trouble getting reviews on your books, even with thousands of people on your mailing list, then go back and work on your foundations.

This book will deal with the points described in parts 2 and 3.2.

FIVE

The Trifecta Of Mailing List Rules

IF THERE ARE ANY "RULES" that govern the long-term success or otherwise of mailing lists, they are these:

1. Mandate
2. Purpose (that's in line with the mandate)
3. Delivery (in line with the list's purpose)

Mandate

The people on the list should understand what they signed up for. Be clear when they sign up: is your list an author newsletter, a new-releases-only list, a list that advertises cross-promotions? Say so when people sign up.

It could easily be that later on, you want to change the focus and branding of the list. In this case, you no longer have a mandate and it's best to ask for people to re-confirm their mandate.

Purpose

Do you want to sell books, inform people, keep a chatty conversation, talk to ARC readers, or talk about your cat? Tell people what you're doing from the outset. Stick to it. They have given you their permission to talk to them about this stuff (mandate).

Delivery

Do as you promised. If you have an author-focused list, and you get bitten by the author cross-promotion bug but now need a place to advertise cross-promotions, start a new list. Don't do this to your existing list. People will get pissed off and report you for spam.

Do the three things above: ask their permission, be clear about what you'll do, and stick to it.

Oh, and if they don't like it, give them a super-easy way out. Put that unsubscribe button at a super-obvious place in flashing neon colours.[1] Yes, people will unsubscribe. This is a good thing.

Pretty simple, right?

To do list:

- If you have a mailing list, examine it in the light of the three principles: mandate, purpose and delivery. I hazard a guess that it's going to look pretty sad. Never mind! We've all been there and done that.

SIX

What Type Of List Do You Have?

IN A VERY BLACK-AND-WHITE kind of world, there are two types of mailing lists. Of course, it isn't quite as simple as stated here, and you can have both types of lists, and there definitely is crossover; but for the sake of the argument, let's keep them separate, at least for a very short time.

The back-end list

This is the type of list that people sign up for when they have read one of your books and get to the end, where they find a link to sign up to be notified when the next book comes out. A back-end list is a *service* to readers. Even more precise: it's a service to existing readers. A back-end list preaches to the choir. You can develop awesome relationships with the people on this list, because they're interested in your books and in you. You can post pictures of your workspace, your holidays, and of your cat. You can post snippets of the book that's about to come out, enlist help from your readers in spreading the word, hold competitions, use your readers' names as characters in books, and so on and so forth. But they're not new and they're already your fans.

The front-end list

The subscribers who join a front-end list often do so because of an incentive. They may part with their email addresses in order to get a free book or in order to take part in a competition. You may have advertised this book or competition solely because it will get people to sign up for your list.

Subscribers of a front-end list typically have not read many of your books (or indeed any of them). Obviously, this limits the type of things that will be attractive to them. However, they are also excellent subjects for pimping books.

While there are obvious differences in the two list types, there are also similarities. Both types of lists will be heavily populated with people interested in books, and, if you have done your homework and placed a few safeguards, even the people who entered just to win a Kindle will be interested in your genre.

So some things you will need to do differently for the list types and some will be the same. And you know what? No one says that you can only have one type. You can have both types of lists on the same account. In fact, I recommend that you do so.

Let's look at the different types of lists, sign-ups, inherent qualities and possibilities.

To do list:

- What type of list(s) do you have?
- What are the unique characteristics of each?

SEVEN

The Back-End List

BY BACK-END LIST, we mean a list where people sign up from a link in the back of your book. By definition, this means people have read and presumably liked that book. They want to know when the next book comes out, and are interested in you as a writer.

Most of this book will deal with incentivised, or front-end, sign-ups, so this chapter will contain most of what I'll say about organic, back-end sign-ups.

And I truly don't need to say much about the subject, because people understand back-end sign-ups. These are your fans. They don't need an incentive to sign up. They have read your work and want to know about you.

Most authors, even many of the traditionally published ones, have a list like this. They notify their fans of new releases. Sometimes they also send newsletters with personal details. Some authors have elaborate structures such as street teams and Facebook groups for fans. I'll say a bit more about these later. They have rallied a keen group of readers who review their books and buy the newest book as soon as it is out.

These people are gold and you need to treasure them.

There are also unlikely to be many of them, at least at first, and their numbers grow very slowly.

It's a rough average that you get about one review for every hundred sales. I have not seen any stats on sign-ups, but you are likely to get fewer sign-ups for every hundred sales. It's a slow, slow business.

What can you do to increase back-end sign-ups?

I have seen some authors have great success with giving them an offer of a bonus story that explains some aspect of the book they've just read. The story will typically only appeal to those who read and liked the book, and the offer will only be made at the end of the book.

Another way to get people to sign up is to make people feel special about being on the list. Give the list and its members a name. Ask them special questions and give them special tasks. Often authors know these people quite well.

These are your early reviewers, your last-minute typo hunters, your beta readers. These are people who will come to your book signings, come to your stand at shows, people who will truly delight and maybe even embarrass you with their fandom. I mean—we all suffer impostor syndrome, and I'm not *that* good to deserve this treatment, am I?

Seriously, these people are awesome, wherever in the world they are.

Treat them well.

One of the major drawbacks of back-end sign-ups is that this method won't give you a workable list within a reasonable amount of time if your books are not selling like hotcakes. The premise of this book is that you want to use your mailing list to sell books. Since subscribers to a back-end list accrue slowly *and* are much more likely to have all your books already, this type of list is a poor candidate for generating sales except for the occasions when you have a new release. I'll have more about this in a chapter on open rates, later.

The reality is that authors who want to use their list to generate sales will *need* to accrue front-end subscribers, or their lists will remain stuck under 100 subscribers, and you can't do much, nor expect much result, from a list that size.

To do list:

- Examine your back-end sign-up process and whether you might be able to increase sign-ups by offering something special related to the book people have just read.

EIGHT

The Front-End List

MOST OF THIS book will deal with front-end lists. This is mainly because if you have chosen to use your mailing list as a way of advertising your books, this is where the biggest potential is.

Back-end sign-ups accrue slowly, especially in the beginning when you've only got a few books out, and no one knows your name. Your list has no serious advertising potential if there are only a hundred people on it. For some, even that may sound like a lot.

If you want to use your list to sell books, you need a significant number of people on it, and front-end sign-ups are the way to go. With front-end sign-ups, you can quickly increase your list to a size that you can do something with, which allows you to evaluate the results.

So what are front-end sign-ups?

These are the people you get on your mailing list as a result of an activity that requires them to leave their email address in return for a benefit. This could be as simple as an incentive to sign up so that they can get one or more of your books for free. Or it could be something as elaborate as a joint promotion with other authors, where you pool your money to give away a fairly large prize, like a Kindle, and collect the entrants' email addresses.

There are many varieties of non-organic sign-ups, and in this book we will discuss a number of them, their effectiveness and things you have to look out for.

While it is true that the subscribers you get this way don't know you from a bar of soap, it is also true that they have given you a mandate to email them. These people are your custom audience. They have parted with their email address in order to get something of yours.

You will probably have heard a lot of preconceptions about these types of sign-ups and promotions, and we will discuss them next. However it is absolutely true that with a bit of work, enough of these people can be turned into loyal readers to make recruiting them worthwhile. Note that the operatives in this sentence are "work" and "enough of these people."

Let's hunt a few more preconceptions first.

To do list:

- Consider the different methods of front-end sign-ups in terms of your own list. What would you be prepared to do now, and what may need to wait?

NINE

Let's Kill Some Dangerous Preconceptions

…RIGHT HERE, before I go any further, let's kill some preconceptions and assumptions that can be quite harmful to your overall mailing list strategy.

If people sign up for your list organically, they have read all your books

Nope. And nope. Not even on your pure, 100% back-end list. Especially if you have more than one series. They may have read the books in that series, with the emphasis on "may". They may have read one book, or all of them. If they haven't read all of your books, then why did they sign up to be notified of the next one? Good question, but people are people and people sign up for mailing lists for all sorts of weird and wonderful reasons.

If you're in doubt about how many books, and which ones, people have read, ask them. People love answering questions, and a survey doesn't do your engagement rate any harm. Use Google Forms or a free account on SurveyMonkey.

People who sign up for a free book only want free books

Nope. Sure, some of them do, but don't worry about those

people. In fact, get rid of them as soon as you've worked out who they are. It's about the people who like getting free books as an introduction to a new author. Those are the ones you want to keep.

If you do giveaways, your list open rate will plummet and unsubscribes will soar

They may, for a little while, or they may not. It depends on where you sourced your sign-ups. It also depends on how well you weed your list out, and how engaging your emails are. Furthermore, I will show you later in this book that nervously checking open and click rates, and making decisions solely based on them, is not productive. So it may or may not be true, but it's actually not terribly important.

The subscribers you get from giveaways are yours

Nope. Non-organic sign-ups have given you one thing: their mandate to email them. It's up to you to engage them. Have a good first free book, and enough of them will buy the second one to make it worth your while.

People who sign up organically are going to be yours forever

Nope. No matter how they signed up, you will still have to keep giving them what you promised to keep their interest. Later in the book, I'll write about mailing list decay, but you'll also need to understand about the honeymoon period, so let's tackle that first . . .

To do list:

- What are your preconceptions?
- Which barriers are you putting in your own way and what is your rationale for maintaining them?

TEN

The Honeymoon Period

I ALWAYS FIND IT surprising that so few people talk about and acknowledge the influence of the honeymoon period on your sales, on a new release or a new list.

Here are some examples of how it applies to your fiction and to mailing lists:

- When your book is new, and if it started selling without much of your involvement, it will keep doing so for a while, but inevitably the newness will wear off and readers will move onto something else.
- When someone joins a new mailing list, they are more likely to open the first emails than they are when they have been on the list for a while.
- When you advertise your new Facebook group, a few people will join and keep conversations going, but unless you get involved, they won't keep doing this. The novelty wears off and they move somewhere else.

The underlying principle is the following: as humans we are

programmed to want churn. When something is new, we find it wonderful and use it, talk about it, and get involved all the time; but after a while, it is no longer new and exciting. It becomes more comfortable and a bit more pedestrian, and unless the thing or activity keeps delivering awesome new content, people are going to look for something else new.

This happens with everything and everybody, like it or not.

Even marriages.

How does this apply to mailing lists? Well, when people have just joined, whether they did so organically or not, they are more likely to open your emails. After a while, you'll find that the people who joined a few months ago are not opening your emails as often anymore.

There is a "catch-em-while-they're-hot" quality about this. During those first few months people are most likely to buy your books and become fans.

So let's get into this part of the process.

ELEVEN

The Main Tools For Getting Sign-ups

THE NUMBER ONE *tool for getting people to sign up is your book*

Remember how in *Self-publishing Unboxed*, I spent the first few chapters talking about your book, its quality and attractiveness, and genre appropriateness? This is why. You need to put out the best book possible, so people will *want* to sign up to read more when it's available. You need to put out the best book possible, even if you're going to give it away for free to new mailing list subscribers.

This book is your honey to attract the bees.

Don't give out a short story with a rubbish cover that has nothing to do with the rest of your work. You can give that once people are your fans. To attract fans, give your best work only.

In the next few chapters, we will go into the different methods you can use to deliver this free book, because some of these offer further opportunities.

Furthermore, when you want to give out a free book, you have to make sure that there are books available for people to buy after they've read the free one, that these books are clearly labelled as part of the same series, and that they're full price and available in as many different places as possible.

The number two tool for getting subscribers is your landing page

I talked a bit about landing pages in *Self-publishing Unboxed*, but I talked more about what's *not* on a landing page, namely anything other than your offer. No menus, no links to other parts of your site, no distractions, nothing.

The primary content of the landing page can be really simple.

Typically, a landing page for sign-ups will display the cover of the book people are going to get, it includes a sales pitch for the book and a field where people can enter their email address and a subscribe button.

Keep the design simple. No busy backgrounds, no strange colours. No orange letters on a black background. Remember that many people will look at these on their phones. Anything that reduces readability has to be eliminated.

KISS: Keep It Simple, Stupid.

The field and the button are an embedded form from your mailing list provider as I described in *Self-publishing Unboxed*, so that when people enter their email address, it is taken straight to your list, at which point your automation sequence will kick in and deliver the free book to them.

I usually only ask for an email address, not a name. Ultimately, whether you have people's names or not doesn't matter in the operation of your list, and people tend to be less likely to sign up the more details you ask them to provide. So: email address and subscribe button—that's all your form needs.

This landing page is your giveaway offer.

Armed with these two tools, you go into the wide world . . .

To do list:

- Before you go any further, re-examine your sign-up form (hosted on your own website as explained in *Self-publishing Unboxed*) and your landing page.
- Does the offer look attractive?
- Does the page look attractive or is it confusing?
- Is it clear what people will get?
- Ask a few people.
- Make sure you update graphics. If your graphics are homemade, pay someone to make an attractive graphic. Poorly made graphics, poor typography, illegible fonts and garish colours can all turn people away. Basically, people don't want to associate themselves with something that they think looks ugly.

TWELVE

Front-End Sign-ups And Their Risk

IN THIS CHAPTER I'll talk about the different ways that you can get incentivised, or front-end, sign-ups. I've divided them into three groups, and will discuss the methods for each. I also talk about the "risk" associated with each of these methods. For this purpose, the term "risk" refers to recruiting the wrong type of people to your list: people who never open your emails or are not the right audience, or people who are likely to report you for spam.

Give away one or more books for free

This is the simplest and some would say the most harmless way of getting people to sign up to your mailing list non-organically.

Grab the URL of the landing page that details your sign-up offer, and put a link to that page in the sidebar on your website, or in the front of your book—and remember how I told you to put the sign-up for your mailing list in front of your book as well as the back? This is why.

Put it in your website's header, in pinned posts in your social media accounts. Put it in a pop-up form that comes up when people visit your website. Yes, I can hear you gasp right now, "Everyone hates those things!"

Do they? Why do so many websites have them? Do you want subscribers or are you afraid to show people the awesome book they can get for free?

Try it, and see if it works.

On my website, I have chosen to put the sign-up graphic in the page header, because I found it more elegant than a popup and couldn't see a major difference in sign-ups, but there may be a difference for you. Try it.

This type of non-organic sign-up can still be quite passive. You can just put a link on your website, on your Facebook author page, on your Twitter profile, and wherever else you are active on social media or elsewhere on the Internet. You can even have it printed on business cards or flyers you give away at cons. The possibilities are endless.

As well as passive, this method of getting non-organic sign-ups is relatively harmless or idiot proof because, although they have not read your books, the people who sign up have already visited your book's page, your profile or your website. They are people who are likely to be at least somewhat interested in what you write.

Free book incentives with advertising

It could be that even when you're giving away a free book as I showed you above, your sign-ups are quite slow, because no one knows about you, you have few followers on Twitter and no one visits your website. So you may decide that you want to give your free book offer a bit of a push. You want to advertise your offer. You will pay to advertise the landing page that you have created as described in the previous chapter and *Self-publishing Unboxed*.

There are several ways to do this, which I will address in later chapters. They can be very effective or very ineffective, and very expensive or very inexpensive, and everything in between.

Again, the people you recruit in this way most likely won't have read your books, but in addition, they have probably never heard of you. They saw "free books" and thought "goodie!" They came over and downloaded the book.

They may indeed only be interested in free books, but you don't know that yet. They are at least interested in books and probably in your genre, because you would have targeted genre readers with the placement of your ad. Or your covers, if done properly, would advertise what sort of books they are. People would self-select. If you write romance, people looking for crime books would not download your freebies and you would not get their email addresses.

With this method, there is obviously a little bit more risk involved, namely that you attract readers who only want free books, but this is still a very good method of recruiting people to your mailing list.

Giveaways and competitions

This is the most high-risk method of recruiting subscribers, even if it can also be one of the most effective. But you have to know what you're doing, and you have to be really careful in selecting the giveaway organisers that you are willing to work with.

The giveaway has to be related to reading, related to your genre, and preferably organised by another author in your genre. It's best if the prize is genre and/or reading related. Giveaways for gift cards and iPads might attract a lot of entrants, but you get a fairly high number of people in these who have never read a book in their lives. You want to avoid those giveaways.

The best giveaways are for books in your genre—because who would want to win books if they never read?

You also have to be quite careful with importing the resulting subscribers lists into your email provider, especially if your list is still quite small. I will say more about importing subscribers later.

I would not recommend you jump into this method straight away because it can get you into hot water. I would also say the method does not make much sense if you have only one or two books out. You need books for them to buy when they have read the freebie, because otherwise you remove the immediacy of recommending something to them that they can buy right now. Remember the honeymoon period? You want the honeymoon period for subscribers to this list to coincide with a period where you have as many books for sale as possible.

I've been doing competitions since 2014 and a large section of my mailing list was built that way. With careful weeding, you can absolutely find new readers who become loyal fans.

To do list:

- Decide which incentive you'll use for front-end sign-ups.
- Make graphics and sign-up pages.

THIRTEEN

Subscriber-Adding Shortcuts

ALTHOUGH I MENTIONED in the previous chapter that using incentivised sign-ups with advertising is more risky than simply waiting for people to sign up by themselves, it is also a very powerful method of quickly building your list.

It is especially useful if you're starting out, you don't have many readers, you are launching something new or you want to start a new list.

In the next few chapters, I will give some ideas of methods, both free and paid, to increase incentivised sign-ups. Your tools will be your landing page and your free books.

The question remains: how do you get your free books to the subscribers?

Please don't attach the book to an email. They may be reading their email on their phone, where it's cumbersome to deal with attachments. They may not want the book on their computer, where they receive email. They want it where they read it.

For several reasons, it's much better to upload the book somewhere and include a link in your email. This way, you can track who clicks which links.

But where? Your website is a possibility, but not all providers allow EPUB or MOBI files to be uploaded. You could use Smashwords and provide the subscribers with a code to get the book free, or you could use another platform like Payhip or Selz, where you can both sell your book or make it free.

Unfortunately, with all these options, which are free to use, you will get no end of questions about how people get their books onto their devices. By the time you've helped two or three people, you will be thoroughly sick of answering this question. You need something easier.

Helping people get freebies onto the device of their choice is exactly what Bookfunnel does best. It was set up with the specific aim to help writers deliver free books to their readers. It offers help files, an app and a response from a real human if your readers are still having trouble. No, it's not free, but it's worth not having to deal with the hassle.

To do list:

- Think about how you will deliver the free books to your subscribers.
- Get accounts at whatever places you choose.
- Upload the books, covers and descriptions.
- See what the download page looks like.
- Copy the links.

FOURTEEN

Free Methods To Add Subscribers

SOME OF THE BEST methods to get people to sign up for your list are free. The catch is that they usually involve some work on your part, but they don't cost you any money either, so that's ideal for authors who don't sell much yet.

All these methods revolve around the same tactic. The landing page and sign-up form you have created in the previous chapter will be your tools. Basically, you will throw these links out everywhere you go, and then make an effort to put them in places you don't normally get to.

You could ask a fellow author to feature you on their blog. In a guest post, you could talk about your books, some specific area of knowledge that you've gained through research, or anything that takes your fancy. At the end of the post you put a link to your free book sign-up page with the recognisable image from the cover of your book that subscribers can get free.

I hope you now see that getting this promotional image right and recognisable is important. The saying goes that people need to have seen an offer seven times before they act on it. Make sure they see it. Use an attractive image.

Of course don't forget to put the same image into your pinned post on any social media platforms where you are active.

You can ask other authors to display your free book offer for you, while you display theirs. You can ask them to feature you or your free books in their newsletter, while you do the same for them.

You can organise a Facebook party and ask other authors to take part in it. In this type of activity, you allocate each author a slot of time for the party, and you'll be at the party's site at your allocated time, talking to readers, giving away prizes, like free books, talking about your books, interviewing others.

By doing this with other authors you pull all your audiences together so that you have a better chance of attracting a good number of people.

Another free resource you can use is Goodreads, where there are groups especially for free books and promotions. Do not promote outside the allocated promotion areas, but you will find groups where it's OK to give out free books.

Here's a trick that helped me gain about a thousand subscribers when I first started my list.

Create a promotional account on Twitter. Please don't do this on your regular personal account where you chat about the weather and your cat, because it will probably turn those people off.

At this virgin promotional account, get a subscription to a service called TweetJukebox. The basic level of subscription is free. It allows you to load a number of interesting tweets in the jukebox which it then automatically repeats as often as you set it for.

Promotions for your books are not examples of interesting posts, although there is nothing wrong with including a few of those. You want posts that people find interesting that are related to either your books or reading. They are likely to be posts by other people. Make sure you include the Twitter handles of those people, so that they know that you have done this for them.

Armed with this account, you start following people. How do you do this?

You go to the Twitter profile of an author in your genre and look at their followers. You follow people who state specifically that they are readers and that they love the genre or they love books in general. Try to avoid other authors for now.

On Twitter it's normal practice for people to follow you back. And when they do this, once a day you go through their profiles and @reply to them, saying, *Hello, here is a link to the page where you can get free books.* Don't send a direct message. Most people find this annoying, and the good thing about an @reply is that a lot of the people will retweet it and in that way you reach their friends too. A lot of people who identify themselves as voracious readers online don't have a lot of money so they love getting free books. I built my first thousand subscribers using this method.

It does take a bit of time, because you seek out the people manually. You don't grab an app that will just auto-follow everyone, because you fill your follow quota with junk accounts very quickly. You have to go to their profiles and read them. Spend half an hour or so each day doing this and you will find your list growing quickly.

But a time will come that you are simply too busy, or that growing your list for as little cost as possible is no longer an objective, and you may want to pay to get subscribers.

To do list:

- Put links to your sign-up landing page in your bio or pinned posts on social media sites.
- Put a link in the sidebar or header of your website.
- Consider using a popup form.
- Find groups on goodreads that allow you to promote free books.

FIFTEEN

Paid Ads

PAID PROMOTIONS work under exactly the same principle as the free ones. The only difference is that you pay to display your ad.

This is where you're going to have to be quite careful because you can spend a lot of money for not much return.

As an author, you're going to be at a disadvantage. Paying for ads puts you on the same field as the large commercial companies. On platforms like Google AdWords or Facebook, you will be competing against the likes of Coca-Cola and Toyota. Because they are selling in much bigger volumes, or sell products that are worth a lot more, and have bigger advertising budgets, it's extremely important that you target your ad very narrowly.

Before you start advertising, you must work out how much you are willing to pay per new subscriber, or how much you're willing to spend on testing per month. Without this limit, costs can escalate very quickly. You also need to set a benchmark for performance of your ads. I suggest that this would be a certain number of new subscribers per month. You should also have a reasonable idea what these subscribers are going to be worth to you. Once they download your free books, how many books are they likely to buy?

Ways to determine this are:

- How many books have your current subscribers bought per person?
- What is the sell-through on your series on retailer sites?

Unfortunately, I've seen figures and formulas mentioned, but I don't believe any of them calculate this accurately. I don't even think it *can* be calculated accurately, especially if you're talking about attracting subscribers from a platform where you have never advertised before. These people will be different from those already on your list.

You can survey the people on your list to ask them how many books they've bought, but whether a statistically reliable number of people respond remains to be seen. I tend to think that this group will heavily self-select in the direction of having bought more books, because those who haven't bought any won't be filling out the survey.

Sell-through on retailer sites will be messed up by the fact that you give book 1 away to subscribers on a different site. It will also be clouded by the fact that some of those sales were generated by the retailer recommendations to people who are not on your list.

So whatever figure you arrive at, even if the hardness of the numbers seems infallible to you, will always be extremely rubbery.

I would simply determine a figure I'd be willing to spend as a promotional budget, a figure I don't *have* to make back, although of course if the ads are no good I won't be continuing them!

It's an experimental promotional budget. How much are you willing to spend for a look-see that may work fantastically, but, at least initially and until you figure out how to target people, may not work at all?

British crime writer Mark Dawson built his list entirely from incentivised sign-ups advertised through Facebook. He was so successful that he now gives courses on the subject. These are well worth checking out, by the way, even if just from the perspective of how ad targeting works.

Some people hit the jackpot and do great on Facebook. Most people, however, are unwilling to put either the time or money into it to make it work. And yes, pay-per-click ads are highly likely to need both of those things.

Of course, Facebook is only one way of advertising your free books-sign-up page. You can also advertise on Twitter, Pinterest, Instagram, even YouTube. There are specialised courses on each of the social media sites. However, I would not go into this unless I had a sizeable backlist to make back the inevitable cost of advertising and the increased cost of running a larger mailing list.

You may be better off writing another book. Maybe. That's up to you to determine. I definitely wouldn't be spending lots on pay-per-click ads if I had only a few books out. Unless, of course something started working really well. And that is why you try it regularly. Dip your toes in once every six months or so. Set a budget, read up on the latest tactics and simply test it.

Other than pay-per-click ads I would look carefully into paid advertising options that are specific to your genre. Not only are they often cheaper, but they come with the added benefit that they're already targeted. There is a site called Project

Wonderful where you can display your ads on a variety of creative comics, genre fiction and reader sites. Ad costs are mere pennies. Maybe you could ask book bloggers if they are open to ads in return for payment.

If you don't want to run your own Facebook ads, there are some companies that advertise that they can do it for you. Yes, it works. Yes, it's very expensive, because you'll be paying for that person's time as well as the ads. And nothing is guaranteed about the quality of the subscribers. I know nothing is guaranteed about the quality of subscribers you get in a giveaway either, but they're likely to cost you less than $50 in total, not $10 per day for an entire month.

So: paid ads—tread with extreme caution.

To do list:

- Decide if you want to pay to drive people to your sign-up page at this point in time.
- Watch Mark Dawson's videos on advertising on Facebook.
- Read a book or two, or check out websites about getting email sign-ups through paid traffic.

SIXTEEN

Competitions And Giveaways

A VERY EFFECTIVE way to gain new subscribers is to do giveaways or competitions with other authors.

In a group giveaway, everyone in the group puts money together to buy a decent prize; and in order to enter and win the prize, people have to part with their email address and sign that they are happy to hear from the authors who have subsidised the prize. The authors then use their individual social media footprint to advertise the giveaway.

Often giveaway organisers will also advertise the giveaway in places where they have to pay for it; for example, they may run Facebook ads or advertise on other platforms.

At the end of the giveaway, the organiser distributes the list of email addresses to the participating authors.

Group giveaways like this will sometimes get a bad rap amongst authors, but they can be a very effective and cheap way of building your list, providing you understand a few things about them:

- By design, these subscriber lists are drawn from the

aggregate of all the lists of the authors involved, so you have to make sure that you don't keep participating in promotions with the same people over and over again.

- In choosing a giveaway to participate in, it is very important that you take part in giveaways that are targeted to your genre and to readers, and don't just give away a monetary prize. You also have to make sure that the person running it has a good reputation, because if you don't, you may get into a lot of trouble. In general I advocate that a couple of close friends in your genre are completely safe, as long as the giveaway states clearly what people are signing up for. In general also, people who sign up for these things know what they get themselves into.
- If this is your first time taking part, you will likely attract more unsubscribes than you have been used to. The people who take part in these gigs are usually savvy and they know the schtick. If they don't want to be on you list, they know how to unsubscribe and will do this. It's not the serial competition-entrants-unsubscribers you need to fear. They will take themselves off the list. It's the people who unwittingly sign up, and then fly into a rage because they didn't read the conditions of entry, and report everyone for spam. Unfortunately, you will always get some of those, so be prepared.

There are also companies that organise these giveaways commercially. They will usually pay for advertising of the promotion on their website. You do have to be a bit careful with these, because not all have great reputations. Unfortunately, there are no metrics that you can easily test. You can ask how subscribers are sourced, but the company can be as detailed, vague, truthful or evasive in their replies as they want. The best way to find out if a company you plan to use is good is to ask other authors.

Also many of these companies will also collect subscribers' email addresses for their own purposes as well as for you. And they will put your email address on their list and keep sending you reminders about their great offers once every day or so. So be prepared for this.

But overall, presuming you have the safeguards in place, competitions and giveaways are great.

There is, however, another method of gaining subscribers at a great rate . . .

To do list:

- Join Facebook groups for cross-promotion for your genre.
- If you don't know of any such groups, go to the Kindleboards or other self-publishing forums and ask.
- Simply ask around, but be clear in what you want: you want groups for authors to coordinate cross-promotions, not groups where people come to spam their books.

SEVENTEEN

Cross-promotion tools

CURRENTLY, IN 2019, writers have a few tools available that are extraordinarily useful for getting subscribers. I have no idea how effective they will remain in the future, or even how many of these tools there will be, but at the moment they are by far the cheapest way of obtaining front-end subscribers for your email list, using your free books.

These are the websites like Prolific Works (formerly Instafreebie), Bookfunnel, Story Origin and My Book Cave.

How do they work?

Well, you open an account, upload your free books and their covers, and create giveaway links. The services are integrated with MailChimp and MailerLite, so enter the list where you want the email addresses of people who download the free books to go.

Then go and join one of the many author cross-promotions. To find these, the sites now list the available group promotions. Most of these promotions have a Facebook group attached where the organisers (who are usually just private authors) will post about the promotion and upcoming activities. When the promotion starts, the service will put all the free books with cover images on a page on their site and all participating authors will advertise that page to their audience.

At the time of writing, all these services are in constant flux and are always updating their range.

At the very basic end, they allow you to upload a book where readers can download it for free without you having to tell them how to sideload it onto their devices.

Cross-promotions are an extension of this service, because if you can attract a lot of people to a page with the lure of a selection of free books, more people will come.

Other than that, all the services are slightly different. Prolific Works has their own audience and newsletter, Bookfunnel allows you to integrate their book delivery service with an online store on your website, Story Origin has a very wide range of promotion options. The promotion page can link to external retailers. My Book Cave allows authors and readers to rate their book for content.

Visit the websites to check them out.

Of course the new people who join your list via these services don't know much about you, but why would these people go to a website that specialises only in free ebooks if they weren't readers of ebooks? They're book enthusiasts, and you can't possibly find a better audience to advertise to. If they're at all inclined to spend money on books—and you have to accept that not all are—these are the people you want to reach.

In order to introduce yourself, you have your welcome automation sequence that kicks in as soon as the email addresses are added to your list. In a series of emails, you can give them more free books, tell them who you are and what you write, and make attractive offers to them. You can be entertaining and funny and review books and send them the things they like.

By giving you their email address these people have given you the mandate to entertain them. Do your best to make them your fans.

To do list:

- Get accounts at Instafreebie and/or Bookfunnel.
- Then go back to those cross-promotion Facebook groups and join group promotions.

EIGHTEEN

Community

I WANT TO SAY an extra few words about cross-promotions and the author community.

Community is extremely important in a solitary pursuit such as writing. Of course you don't have to connect with anyone, and you don't even have to leave the house, but often the writers who connect with some kind of community, whether in real life or online, do better than those without.

You need community. Even a group of writer friends can be an enormous help. They will answer your questions, share your frustrations and understand your triumphs. These groups are where you find out the tricks and you find out where the cross-promotions are organised, because a lot of them are not found in a formal setting that you can search for. Quite often you may even need to be invited into these communities, which means that you need to know someone who is already in them, and need to have shown to these people that you are willing to commit and do the work required.

The self-published author community is particularly strong and the cross-promotions, whether for sales or for mailing list sign-ups, are proof of this. At any one time, in any number of Facebook groups, you can find promotional teams that you can join with your books. Some of them will use cross-promotion services, some link to retailers because they're group sales. Whatever the case, join some of these and be a good member of the community. Not only is the network between authors strong, reputation is a precious thing. If you show yourself willing to help others, others will help you in return.

Do the right thing by your fellow authors, and they will remember you.

If you give freely within the community, you will benefit from that later.

To do list:

- Consider your role in the author community and whether you are a good citizen.
- If you subscribe to cross-promotions, keep a calendar to make sure that you don't forget to honour commitments you made.
- Make sure that you read the guidelines of any promotion or group and stick to them, and don't ask for special consideration. Few organisers get paid for their jobs. They're just fellow authors. Don't punish their time commitment by being annoying.

NINETEEN

Importing Addresses

SO YOU HAVE TAKEN part in a competition and the organiser has just sent you a list with two thousand subscribers. What do you do with them?

It will depend a bit on how big your list is, and this is one of the reasons that I tell you not to take part in giveaways unless you have an established list. Most email providers don't actually like you importing lists of people, because the behaviour is so similar to someone buying lists illegally somewhere off the Internet, people who did not give their permission.

To your provider, your track record is going to be extremely important in determining whether to deliver your emails and whether they will even let you import the list.

So if this is your first time doing it, you have to be very careful. I suggest you do this only after you have been with your email list provider for a few months and have established a good track record.

I am going to assume that you have been careful how you determined which giveaway to take part in. Don't let yourself be lured by the prospect of getting thousands of addresses. At this point, it is better to get a few hundred and be cautious.

If you did happen to get two thousand addresses, you're happy that they were properly acquired, and your list is still small, I would split them into three or four groups before importing. Make the first group the smallest.

Certain email providers will already have a master list of banned email addresses of people who are known to cause problems. These will be fake emails, spammers, sellers of addresses and serial spam reporters. This is a game of give and take, and some people take way more than they give. There's no pleasing them, and it is in no one's interest to have these people on their list. They will filter them out for you.

I would suggest that you make a new list for your new giveaway subscribers. Usually, the organiser sends you a spreadsheet. Open the spreadsheet in whatever program you use to open spreadsheets. Then I usually just copy and paste the column with the email addresses from the spreadsheet. Unless you have asked for people's names—which I don't until people have been on my list for a while—there's no need to copy all the other information. Copying and pasting from a spreadsheet gives a more hassle-free importing of data than trying to get the program to import your entire file in one go.

You may consider giving the new subscribers a tag which tells you how they joined, either by putting them in a separate list that you name after the competition, or by adding a custom field to their addresses. However if you have done a couple of these giveaways, you will see that there are a lot of repeat email addresses of people who take part in these giveaways all the time, and keeping track of all the competitions can be very daunting, dare I say "too much information".

To be honest I just dump them all in what I call a competitions portal, which is a list that I use for people I have just imported, but are not on any of my other lists, and that I will need to sort into useful and less useful addresses.

Whichever way you do it, after you have imported them, start them on an automation sequence. I also make sure that this automation sequence doesn't start straight away, but with a delay of an hour, in case I make a stupid mistake and I need to reverse it. It may sound unlikely to you now, but I have definitely imported the wrong list of people into the wrong email sequence.

What is important, however, is that once these people are on your list, you send them something as soon as possible. Some of the giveaways stipulate that each author should send them something on an allocated date. In that case do as you have been told, because by being a good citizen, you will be invited to take part again.

If there is no such stipulation, send an email to these people as soon as possible. Remind them of the competition, why they are on your list, and then introduce yourself. At this point, most writers also find it a good idea to give away a free book, even if you haven't already started them on your sequence where they get the books you normally give out free to your list.

I would also suggest that at this point you make it clear to these people where they can unsubscribe. Yes, getting a bunch of unsubscribes may hurt a little, but I can tell you that you don't really want people on your list who don't want to be there. For one, you are paying for them.

Repeat this process with each of the list segments that you have made, until they are all in your list. Breaking up a large batch of subscribers potentially makes you aware of any problems with the group. If you got these addresses from a promotion between authors, you are not so likely to see a lot of problems. But if you have used a commercial company for your giveaway, you should be a little bit more cautious. If you see an unusually high percentage of unsubscribes or spam reports from the first group, I would advise against importing the rest. I would also make a note never to use that company again.

Importing lists becomes much less risky when your list grows, because by the time you have five thousand subscribers, importing a list of a thousand is not such a big deal. Also, by that time, you already have a history with your provider.

In general, the providers hate it when you open a new account and then start importing large lists of subscribers. This is for their own protection. If you import a troublesome list on a virgin account, they'll just shut you down without argument. If you've been a trouble-free customer of theirs for a while, you get a bit more leeway.

To do list:

- If it's your first time importing a list, divide it into a couple of batches.
- Send the first batch an email and wait to see what the reaction is.
- Send the next one when the first batch doesn't present any problems.

TWENTY

What Next?
_____

SO NOW THE PEOPLE are on your list. What do you do next?

Here is where you should probably make a clear distinction between the people on your back-end list and the ones on your front-end list. The ones on your back-end list may have signed up just to get new releases. You will have promised this in your sign-up process. Most writers don't release something new every two weeks. The people on your organic list know that, and they are happy to receive something from you every couple of months. They're not going to forget about you in that time. Or they have signed up for a newsletter, a chatty email from you on a regular basis—as you promised them—and you write about project updates.

People on your front-end list however, have no idea who you are yet. And what's more, if you don't email them immediately, they are highly likely to have forgotten the competition they took part in that put them on your list. So as I said in the previous chapter, you should email them immediately, reminding them of the competition, where they signed up, and introduce yourself and your books. Leaving this too long will cause you grief. *Don't* just import them into your personal author list that you only email when you have a new book out.

If you're going to get front-end people, they will mean WORK for you.

You have to email them. You have to engage them. You have to sell yourself.

You should give them an easy way to unsubscribe. I know, it hurts to have 100 people unsubscribe from one email, having your ego crushed in 100 parts with each unsubscribe notice. Really, do all of you guys hate me that much?

One notion you should throw out of the window right now is that these people were yours to start off with. They never were. They took part in a giveaway. They didn't mind that a consequence of being in the giveaway was that you were going to email them.

They are NOT your fans. They are NOT your people.

Unsubscribes are part of running a list. Unless they suddenly spike out of the ordinary, you do best to ignore them. People unsubscribe for as many weird reasons as they subscribe. People are weird. Be prepared.

Actually, if your email provider sends you one of these cheery emails when people subscribe or unsubscribe, go in and turn off that feature right now. It's annoying and messes with your head.

I can assure you, getting a hundred unsubscribes is better than getting spam reports or carrying thousands of people on your list who have no interest in being there. In fact, I'll be even more blunt: once people from competitions and giveaways are on your list, you should view your list as a tree that you give a good shake every now and then so that the rotten apples fall out. Give the people who have no interest in you every opportunity possible to unsubscribe.

So that is a major difference between the two lists. You have to email a list from a non-organic sign-up much more frequently. You have to do work to sort out the people who want to be there and are useful for you, and do your utmost best to get rid of the rest.

If you remember what I said in the beginning of this book about mandate, you'll have to admit that the mandate these people have given you is a little bit rubbery. They—sometimes begrudgingly—accepted the fact that you were going to email them because they wanted to take part in this competition. They didn't specifically give out that email address because they wanted to hear from you. So it's going to matter a lot more what you do and how you treat them.

The people on your back-end list are going to be happy to be emailed once a week or once a quarter, or however often you have promised them.

The people on the front-end list don't know you and have never heard of your books, but for the most part they are happy to be entertained. So you write a program to entertain them. And this is the major function of mailing list automation.

But first you must remember . . .

To do list:

- Examine your unsubscribe link and see if you can customise it or the displayed text.
- Can you put it in a prominent place?

TWENTY-ONE

The Ultimate Function Of Your List

CLASS, WHAT IS the ultimate function of your mailing list?

If you said, "To own your audience," you get 50 points, but full marks go to those who said: "To sell your books."

Oddly enough, this fact almost always gets lost in the discussion of mailing lists. Authors start mailing lists because other people say that you should.

Fact of life: never do anything because someone else says so if you don't understand why you should do it.

A mailing list is not an ego trip, it's not a subject to boast about how engaged they are—although power to you if you do have such a list.

A mailing list is an advertising vehicle, and a pretty powerful one at that.

Think about it:

If I gave you the choice between spending $100 to pay a company to send notice of your new book or special to 10,000 people, every month, or spending $1200 to acquire a mailing list of 10,000 email addresses to whom you can then send whatever you want, because they're yours, the choice would be simple.

But few people see it that way. They see the mailing list as a *service* to readers, not a vehicle to sell books.

Mark Dawson calls it "building your own Bookbub": creating, over time, an audience, a significant percentage of which will buy your new releases, if not immediately, often later. What is more, you can keep the addresses to use again for your next release, and the next one. And if you have no release, advertise a friend's book, append your affiliate code and make a bit of money that way.[1] The people on your list will email you to thank you for these suggestions.

The point of your list is to make money.

Your mailing list is for selling books. This is why I place more emphasis on front-end lists than back-end lists. A back-end list is a service, and a pretty simple one at that: sign up here and I'll notify you when there is a new book. Or: sign up here and I'll send you a monthly newsletter. Easy. Comfortable. We all get it.

But ultimately, in this business, we want to invest time and money into something because we want to sell books. And the front end is where you can sell the most, especially because few of these people will have read any of your books.

Supposing you had twelve books because you were following the Three-Year Plan and wrote twelve books in four trilogies. Supposing you gave new subscribers the first book in each of the trilogies for free, you then have eight books you can sell. Suppose you made $3 from each of those sales, a subscriber can potentially be worth $24. If you then decided that one of the trilogies was popular enough to warrant a second trilogy, all paid, that's another $12, all to people you know and control. Sure, you will send them to a retailer for the transaction, but where you send them becomes irrelevant, except you should probably offer as many different places as possible. It's not your business to dictate where people should buy.

I strongly hope that you can now see that dumping a list that you gained through non-organic methods into a newsletter that you run as a back-end service can end in a lot of tears. These people don't know who you are. Do you really think they will care about your work in progress when they haven't read any of your books?

Similarly, if you get a bunch of subscribers from a giveaway, dump them in your regular list and suddenly go all salesy in your newsletter, this will cause grief with your back-end subscribers.

You can deal with this issue in a number of ways, which we will discuss now.

TWENTY-TWO

Which Program For Which List?

LET'S GET INTO the big question: what do you send people once they've joined your list?

I hope that by now you can see that there is a clear distinction between what's suitable for a back-end list and a front-end list. You should absolutely not send them the same stuff, at least initially.

When someone joins your back-end list through a sign-up at the end of a book, they will want to hear what you specifically promised them. New releases, or a chatty newsletter, whatever it was you told them you'd send them.

But what about the front-end list?

These people may just have downloaded one free book, but not read it, by the time you send them your first email. Those people are not fans of yours, but they can be turned into fans.

You have a number of different options:

- You can send these people through an automation

sequence that introduces them to you and your books, and then import them into your regular list.
- You can keep these people separate and develop a completely separate email strategy for them involving your books.
- They came to your list because they signed up for a competition, so you can send them more competitions, cross-promotions and group sales.

Why would you choose any of these options?

You'd choose the first option for simplicity. If you are going to write just one newsletter to everyone and wanted to promote your own books, you would make sure that new subscribers are familiar with those books before you let them join your regular newsletter.

I'd consider the second option if I had a back-end list that I only sent new release information to. You can't import your front-end people into a new-release-only list. You need to engage them first, or they will unsubscribe en masse with your new release notices, because they have forgotten who you are.

The third option can be very powerful if you are going to take part in promotional events a lot. These events often require that you send information about the promotion to your list. Unless you set up your back-end list with this premise, you don't have the mandate to go promotional on them, so you make a list of the people you get from giveaways. Because people on this list expect to be sent giveaways and promotions, you can advertise your own promotions, too. What is more, you can advertise other people's promotions.

But, why should you advertise other authors' books on a list that you are paying for?

It seems counterintuitive, but in the world of reading and writing, I have found that the more you share and the more you give, the more you get back.

Another reason you may want to do this is to make back, through affiliate sales, the cost of running your list. But to be honest, the percentages are so low that this is not going to be a major moneymaking venture, just a way of defraying the cost of running a list of tens of thousands of people until you sort out which ones to keep, and while you're still not selling very much. Some people then, of course, discover that they like marketing and networking and that they happen to be really good at affiliate marketing, but that is another story.

To do list:

- Consider your email list strategies:
- How many newsletters do you want to send?
- Do you keep a new-releases-only list, or can you integrate your front-end and back-end lists after the front-end people have been through an introduction sequence?
- Do you want to start a separate competitions list?

TWENTY-THREE

Your Email Strategy

NOW THAT YOU have determined why these people are on your list, and what sort of strategy will suit them, you must start thinking about how you're going to entertain them. In other words, what kind of emails are you going to send them?

For your personal back-end list, this is going to be fairly easy. They will be interested in when your next book is out and snippets from your upcoming work in progress and background information and things about yourself or your cat. Never underestimate the power of cat pictures. The Internet is fuelled by cats.

For any non-organic sign-ups, whether they come from cross-promotion services, through Facebook advertising or giveaways, it is a good idea to design an auto responder. This is a handy program that does all the marketing for you. And this is where email becomes really powerful as a marketing tool. There will be a lot more about email automation later.

You have to decide how often you're going to email them. As I already said, if people come from a non-organic source, they are more likely to forget who you are if you don't email them regularly. On the other hand, you don't want to overwhelm them; but I would recommend emailing them no less than twice a month.

There is another reason for doing this. Your first introductory email to a group of competition entrants is likely to attract the highest number of unsubscribes. But even after that first email, the next few emails are likely to report a reasonably high unsubscribe and spam report rate.

One of the metrics that your email provider keeps about you is the unsubscribe and spam report rate per email and it has targets for each. If you breach the target, you'll get a warning.

It may seem counterintuitive, but the more you email them—up to a point of course—the more this rate per individual email goes down. This is for the simple mathematical reason that if you give one group of people three links to click and a second group of people, the same size as the other group, gets only two links, each of the links in the group of three will have a much lower click percentage than the links in the group of two.

So if you have a big list of competition entrants and you want to weed out the ones who don't want to be there, make sure that you email them regularly. If you don't email them they won't unsubscribe. Silly as it sounds, when you import a large competition and giveaway list, from the moment the people are on your list, it is your task to get them to do one of two things: buy your book or unsubscribe.

To do list:

- Determine how often you want to email to which list.

TWENTY-FOUR

Stuff To Send Your List

NOW YOU'RE STUCK with having to send a bunch of strangers an email every two weeks. What on earth are you going to send them?

In the first place, it will have to be something sustainable. Something that you will be able to come up with every two weeks for the foreseeable future. It's not much good committing to sending people something when you're going to run out of ideas after a few emails.

In the second place, unless you've committed to a specials-and-giveaways newsletter, it will have to be something that's probably not too promotional. People are quite sensitive to being sold to, especially if they've already seen the same book pimped before.

If you want your book to sell, you don't tell people how great it is, you show them what's inside it. If you have written a book that includes research about an interesting fact, tell them about what you found, and at the end mention that it is included in the book. Then of course it would be stupid not to include any links to the book in question. Use your book's landing page for this.

Other topics that you can use would be interviews with other authors, descriptions of localities in your books, and photos of those localities.

You can include things about the writing process. People like to know what a writer does. If someone asks you "How do you get your ideas?" write a newsletter segment that answers the question.

If you're comfortable, add tiny bits about your personal life, especially as they relate to writing. You may answer questions such as: How did you start writing? And when did you decide to go full time? In my case, I have a couple of anecdotes about the traditional publishing industry. I love the one where some unnamed person in one of the world's biggest publishing companies told me "You will never sell this book," in those words, about a book I sold immediately after, and that is now part of my highest-earning series. People love that stuff.

People also love a little bit of personal stuff, especially if there is something special about where you live or your situation that will be alien to them. My subscribers get a kick out of when I mention winter in June and July or the fact that we're almost a day ahead of them.

Include things about the daily life of an author. Things that make them laugh. Animals. And never neglect to mention a different book of yours with each email. Always give them a one-click link where they can find all your books on one page. Use this link in your signature line or some other place with each email your send them.

You can already see that if you have only one or two books out, coming up with new and interesting subjects is going to be a real stretch. Beware of subject creep, where for want of material you start talking about—say—movies you watched. In that instance, you have metamorphosised your list into a movie review list, and the people who hang around do so because of your movie reviews. That's fine if you like writing movie reviews, but it detracts from your fiction.

So what do you do if you have few books out? In that case you are probably better off creating a competition list, to which you will send specials, giveaways, and new releases from other authors as well as your own. Because you probably don't have enough material to keep the list occupied and interested for that amount of time. And in turn those other authors may do something for you when you have a new release out.

Setting up a list is easy, but this sort of stuff warrants careful planning.

In fact, you are now editing a newsletter in the same way that news bulletins of old used to work. The editor had to find something interesting for the subscribers with every issue, something that fitted within the newsletter's subject matter and would not alienate subscribers or pull in people from the wrong target audience.

Target audience examples:

- People who read *your* books: write about you, about your books, give them snippets and talk about research.
- People who like your genre: author interviews, pimping your books as well as other authors' books, cross-promotions, book reviews, movie reviews.
- Other writers: craft, business of self-publishing, industry gossip, courses, podcasts
- Freebie and competition junkies: free books, competitions, giveaways, sales.

With each email you write, step back and consider if it addresses the right target audience. If you cross-target a few times, no one is going to bite you, but make sure you nip permanent subject creep in the bud. Because if people like your emails for their movie reviews, then you're going to be mightily disappointed that they won't buy your latest release.

A brief word here about email titles.

It is a fact that open rates vary between different titles. You can find many articles about the subject. For example, the MailChimp help files mention a list of words to avoid. One of the words that affects authors is the word "free". Apparently emails with the word free in the title are more likely to land in junk mail folders. As a personal antidote to the conventional wisdom, I—and I'm not the only author who reports this—usually find increased open and click rates if I use the word free in the email's title.

The bottom line is: don't believe what the all-knowing "they" say until you've tested it and found it so.

One "rule" I have definitely found to be true is that email titles that are plain and simply state what's inside the email have higher open rates than titles that try to be funny or clever. People don't have time for clever, and if you think funny is interpreted the same way around the world, I invite you to watch a show the Brits find funny and one Americans find funny, never mind the rest of the world. "Funny" only applies to a very narrow target audience. Your list is world-wide. People won't get it. If someone doesn't get it, they will feel stupid. One awesome way to disconnect from people is to make them feel stupid.

Also beware that you don't make your emails too long. People are busy and many of them read emails on their phones.

Scrolling through pages and pages of stuff on a tiny screen is no fun.

Personally I have chosen to divide my emails to my author subscription list into a couple of sections. There is an introductory section with current news, often followed by something about research or locality or some other factual knowledge; then I will have a randomly chosen focus book out of my catalogue. This is usually not a first book in a series. I'll have an image of the cover and will include a small paragraph where I talk about the book in a chatty way: about how it was written or what my aim was with the book, instead of just repeating the book's blurb as people can also see it on the retailer sites. Then I often include a free book that's not mine. The people on my list who are still reading by the time they get to the bottom of my email are the ones who have already downloaded and read my free books. Unfortunately I am not a writing machine, and I only publish one book every three months. People can read much faster than that, so I keep them occupied by giving them free books written by my friends. This has proven to be a very good strategy for keeping open and click rates high in my emails. These people come from both back-of-book sign-ups and downloads of my free books.

I also have a mailing list that consists of people whose addresses I got through competitions and giveaways. I send them mostly other competitions, giveaways and group sales once a week, but I also include a focus book in this email. That book is usually mine, and I often advertise my own free books and my own author list to these people. Remember that they took part in a competition and they are not your fans. By advertising my own list to these people, I allow a more organic transition between my competition list and my author list. This keeps the engagement of my author list quite high.

To do list:

- Make a list of topics and ideas to write about.
- Make sure that you keep this list in a handy place (like, your phone) so you can add to it when you get an idea.
- Subscribe to a few lists from fellow authors in your genre to see what they do.
- Read up about email titles. It may be worthwhile deciding on a recognisable format; for example, mention the name of the newsletter each time you send an email.

TWENTY-FIVE

Email Design

AT THIS STAGE, I probably need to say a few things about email design.

Your email list provider (MailChimp, MailerLite etc.) will provide a series of templates that you can use to design your emails. You can drag & drop boxes of text and images. Designs vary from plain white to really busy designs that look like restaurant menus or printed leaflets.

What should you use?

Personally, I'm in favour of a simple design. Remember that many people read these emails on their phones. The templates should be mobile friendly, but you really don't need garish colours and designs that look like you're selling the latest fashion.

But whatever you choose, templates or a simple design, absolutely do the following:

- Get rid of any standard images that come with the design and insert your own
- Get rid of the little graphic at the bottom of the

email that advertises the service. If you have a free account on most of these services, you can't turn this off. Yeah, it makes you look like a cheapskate.
- Get rid of standard displays of social media icons, because every other writer and their cats will be using those same standard settings.

Some other design notes:

- Many of these email services use as standard design grey print on a white background. A lot of people find this hard to read. Change the type to black.
- Don't use light text on a black background.
- Don't, on pain of death, use fancy fonts or Comic Sans in your emails.
- If you're going to insert images, by all that's dear, scale them down to a width of 640 pixels (MailerLite) or 500 pixels (MailChimp) first. Even if you use a picture taken on your phone, it will be 3000 pixels wide and the size is huge, eats up bandwidth, slows down the loading of your email (remember that people read on their phones?) and just annoys the crap out of people.
- Don't use more than 4–5 images per email.
- Make sure all your images are attractive. If you have zero design skills, pay someone to design promotional graphics. Otherwise stick to photographs.
- If you have no design skills, even if you have no money to spend on this, pay someone to make just the header that you will use for each email.

To do list:

- Decide on a template to use for all your emails.

- Clean up all things that advertise your list provider's website.
- Make changes to type, social media buttons and colours and save as a reusable template.
- Get a nice header graphic.

TWENTY-SIX

Introduction To Automation

AUTOMATION IS THE powerhouse of mailing list operation. It allows you to send out messages that you have prewritten, triggered by certain events or actions taken by subscribers. Do you know those messages you get from Amazon about three weeks after you have bought a book, those emails that ask you if you want to review the book? Those are automated messages. So are the ones that you receive about books whose pages you have visited.

Often writers get excited about this. Amazon is sending out reminders that include my books! It's always a little painful to tell them the truth: they get the messages because they have an Amazon account and because they visited those books' pages. It's a simple thing operated through link tracking. Oh, oops. Maybe you should refresh your product page a bit less often.

But my point is that these emails are triggered by your visit to a page. With email automation, you can do that yourself.

Even the most basic email provider will have automation that starts as soon as a subscriber joins a list. You will need this, at the very least.

But there is much more you can do with automation, if given the tools.

For this reason, I recommend that you sign up with an email provider that allows you to trigger automation according to actions taken by the subscriber. For example if they click the link or if they opened an email, or a certain time after they joined your list. Unfortunately none of the providers handle automation and subscribers in the same way. Finding out how to do it in yours may require some lateral thinking.

If you have the option to let automation assign a value to a field in your subscriber's data, then you can do almost anything. It is a matter of finding out how to do it. Unfortunately I can't give a guide how to do this, so you will have to consult your provider's help files. If they are not good, or their help team doesn't respond to your questions, it may be a good idea to look for another place to host your list. Automation will greatly improve the value you get from your list, and there is no need to be hamstrung by crappy services from a crappy provider. Move your list now, before it gets too big.

A warning: automation is not easy. It requires some planning and thought. It may take quite a long time after a subscriber joins a list that it kicks into action. At times, you may need to think about what to do about the people in this queue if you want to change something else. You have to make sure that all the pieces go in the right place. I find that it helps to keep your automation sequences short, because if something goes wrong, you haven't lost a big chunk of information, or you don't have many subscribers missing out on something. It is better to have two automation sequences of five emails each than to have one of ten.

Keeping sequences short is not just a protection against mistakes on your part. Sometimes, a provider will change a system, and inevitably some subscribers will be left in limbo. If you keep your sequences short, this will affect as few people as possible.

In the next chapter I will go through different types of operations that you can perform, with some principles behind them. Unfortunately, I cannot give instructions for each email provider because they are all different, and because they change their systems all the time. I will, however, tell you what operations you should look for.

To do list:

- Design an email sequence of 3–5 emails for people who join your list through competitions and free book giveaways.
- Make sure you use the same header graphic for each.

TWENTY-SEVEN

Your Welcome Sequence

THE WELCOME SEQUENCE is the series of emails people first get when they join your list. In your automation menu, there should be a trigger that's called "when a subscriber joins a list" or some such.

It is a good idea to tailor the sequence to each list, especially if the subscribers come from different sources.

If, for example, you got a list from a competition or a giveaway, it's a very good idea to remind your subscribers that you got their email address because they signed up for the giveaway. I would make the welcome sequence a few emails long. More than one, but I wouldn't send them more than five. Just as illustration, I will briefly describe my process.

As soon as a subscriber joins my author list, they get sent an email which contains images of the covers and the links to my four free series starter books. I use the covers because people can tell the book's genre from them, and if they're not interested in fantasy, they will choose the science fiction ones and vice versa.

Each of those image links takes them to a page on Bookfunnel.

Two weeks later, they get an email that asks them whether they got the free books all right. Before I joined Bookfunnel, this was a necessity, because a lot of people would not know how to get the books onto their devices, and by not checking on them, I would lose a lot of readers because they downloaded the book, but then did not know how to read it.

But I've actually found that this email gets one of the highest response rates of all the emails I send. People will reply saying "Yes I got them, thank you very much". To which I will then reply "Happy reading".

Then in the third email in the sequence, I explain that I'm going to send them into another automated sequence which introduces them to all my series and that if they click on a button they can opt out of this. Under the button is another automation sequence that is triggered by the clicking of the button and that moves the subscribers to another list, bypassing the book introduction sequence. None of this involves anything I need to do.

Whatever process you decide on, in the first email you will typically introduce yourself and your books, and if you give away any free books for joining your list, the first email is typically where you put them. Typically, if people are on your list because they received a free book or they took part in a giveaway, this is the email that will cause the most unsubscribes. This is not a problem for you and you should not fret over it. Those people were simply there for the giveaway or the freebie. Let them be. The fact that they unsubscribed also means that you will not bother them again, no matter how many other giveaways they take part in, because your mailing list provider will not let you re-import people who have unsubscribed.

In this first email, mention how they came to your list. You may mention the name of the giveaway, but if it is an automation that's probably not a good idea, because you will have to change it every time you import people from a different giveaway. Then introduce yourself: who you are what sort of books you write. Keep the introduction fairly short, and add something that might prompt them to click or reply to you. This could be something funny, or a picture of your cat, because people love animals, and in case you didn't know this yet, cats are the driving force of the Internet. I'm joking, of course, but if you include something that people can relate to, they are more likely to open your subsequent emails. They like seeing that you're a real person and not some kind of marketing machine.

Keep the introductory email quite short. People are busy and will disengage if they are faced with a wall of text and too many opportunities.

How long should you leave it before you send the second email?

There are several schools of thought about this. Marketing companies will advise you to email every couple of days. Other writers will be more cautious. I use as a benchmark the frequency Amazon emails readers. If you are on one of their genre email lists, you will know that they send you an email every second week. So my second email to my subscribers in my automated series goes out after two weeks. You can experiment with this, but I feel two weeks is probably a good enough time period.

So, as I said above, after two weeks I send them another email asking if they were able to download my free books correctly. I also like to tell them about how authors appreciate reviews. The point of the second email is to hold people's interest so that they will continue to open my emails, and as a result, my emails are less likely to end up in their promotions folder. People respond well to questions. They like being asked for their opinion. Be creative.

Then, after another two weeks, they get another email with my promise to them. I tell them that I will email them roughly every two weeks and I will give them news and updates on my books. I ask them where they buy their books.

This is my basic welcome automation sequence. There are only three emails, but by the end of those three emails the people who are genuinely not interested will have unsubscribed already.

I do other things with them, which I will describe in later chapters.

TWENTY-EIGHT

Advanced Automations

THE BASIC AUTOMATION sequence I talked about in the previous chapter is the minimum you should have. Most email providers, even the very basic ones, will allow you to set this up.

But in order to have more advanced processes, you will need to be with a provider that offers a little bit more than just automation that's triggered when people join.

You want automation based on when they click a link or automation that can move them to a different group or a segment or give them different tags. Tags are data fields in the line that holds each subscriber's information. It's like a spreadsheet column. In the first column, there is the date that they joined, the next one their email address, then maybe their name. Most providers also offer standard fields for address and phone number and other things that we never use as authors. I don't even use name. But you can add custom fields: another column where you can put whatever you want. So I could make an automation that when a subscriber clicks a link, the software ads a value for a tag. Then you can use the tags to sort people who have clicked certain links and put them into groups or list segments. As I already said, each provider handles this differently and you will have to check the help files of yours.

Tags and list segments are enormously powerful and allow you to search in your subscriber base for people with specific behaviours, like when they downloaded a free book. You can send them to automation sequences just for them, for that particular series or even that particular book.

Remember the first email in my welcome sequence, the one that displays the covers of the four free books with links?

When a subscriber clicks a link, an automation sequence changes the tags to include the name of the books they downloaded.

And a set number of days later, another email goes out automatically, just like Amazon does, asking them if they enjoyed the book and would they be willing to review it? And then I also give them a bit of chatty information about the second book in the series.

All this happens without my involvement.

I do the same for new book releases. When a subscriber clicks that link, my automation sequence makes a note of it, and I can choose to do something with it later.

As I said the opportunities with automation are endless, limited only by your own imagination, and the fact that automation tends to give you a headache just thinking about it.

To do list:

- Set up follow-up automations for free books people received when they signed up.
- Check your list provider's options to see if you can move people into different groups or give them tags based on what they click.

TWENTY-NINE

Other Things

THERE ARE A COUPLE of other things that you can do with the mailing list that I haven't yet talked about.

For example you can give out advanced reader copies, or ARCs. Some people will express their dismay about the fact that some authors, especially those who write Romance, will launch a book and immediately it will have 100 reviews. This while they struggle to get as few as ten reviews in the first year of publication. Getting reviews is not easy, but it becomes a lot easier when you dangle a free book in front of subscribers and ask them to review it for you.

You can recruit these people into a reviewer team. You remember all those people who said they only want free books? Well this is how you use them. Some people are genuinely short of money, they like to read and you help them in this way. They help you and everyone is happy.

Another thing you can do with your list is to hold your own competitions. You will do this as a promotional activity to draw attention to earlier volumes in your series, or just as a fun thing for loyal subscribers. Whichever it is, the notification that people can win something usually does wonders for your open rate of your emails. On several occasions, I have found that the people who win a competition have gone on to read all of my books, or I have maintained another kind of relationship with them. And on a very basic level, this is what a mailing list is about: building relationships.

Another fun thing you can do with your list is to use it for research. This may sound strange, but if you have several thousand people on your list, they will be from all walks of life. They will live all over the world, or have lived in many different places or visited them. There will be people young and old, and people from all different kinds of professions. So if you're writing about something that requires checking by a specific professional, you may just ask your list if there is anyone on it who knows about this specific situation. I have used this several times. For example, I needed to write about a court procedure, and I asked people on my list where I could find information that told me how to write this. I have also asked people on my list to voluntarily enter their profession and email so that if I ever have a question about a certain profession, I can ask them.

Many people are genuinely fascinated by the work of an author, and they are more than delighted to take part.

A very special thing you can do for your most loyal subscribers is to name a character after them. I did this in one of my novels, and it is a lot of fun. Yes, there really is a reader named Lenka Trnkova. There is also a real person named Mobashar Qureshi. People can suggest what kind of character they want to be, whether they mind being a bad guy or whether they mind being killed. It is amazing how many responses I got from women who nominated their ex-husband's name with the note that they want to see him killed as cruelly as possible.

Again, mailing lists are about engagement and asking

subscribers. Questions like this, and having fun with their responses, is what it's all about.

To do list:

- Consider what other things you could do with your list—not just what you could do for them, but what they could do for you.
- Set up an ARC team by starting a new list and asking people from your existing list to join.

THIRTY

Be Creative, Be You

ONCE UPON A TIME, a writer wrote a popular book about how to pick a genre on Amazon US that you were likely to be able to rank in, because there were relatively few books and a lot of readers. He described his methods in detail, but when people followed his advice, a good deal of them missed the step that said, "Find your genre." They wrote in the genre *he* had shown as example.

Once upon a time, another writer had success with Facebook ads. He is a very pleasant, kind dude and showed his successful ads and how to set them up. Lo and behold, a lot of people started doing Facebook ads. But instead of finding their own unique voice, they copied, almost to the word, the text from the example ad.

Seriously, they couldn't even think of their own genre and their own words?

What sort of sheeple are these?

Enter the reason I don't give out basic formats and templates. I do this for a very specific reason. At the level of designing automation, marketing is a creative endeavour. It is up to you to design a sequence and email format that is unique to you. If I gave out templates with guidelines, everyone would be copying them and every email sequence would look the same, because people are lazy and just copy stuff that they're given. I bet that if I gave out templates with tracking links embedded, many people would not even remove these. It's really shocking the degree to which people are copycats.

If there is one thing that I want you to take away from this book, it is: do not be a copycat. Make your stuff memorable.

To do list:

- Put on your thinking hat. Take a piece of paper into the garden or your favourite café and write down the sort of things that you could write about that are related to your fiction. Write down what sort of strategy you're going to use for your list. Write down what you may need in terms of graphics, or input from other people. Draw a diagram of how you want your automation to work. And then find your own way.

THIRTY-ONE

List And Audience Segmentation

A QUESTION THAT comes up frequently is:

I write science fiction and fantasy (or two other genres). Should I have two lists?

My answer to that is going to be infuriating: it depends.

I write in two genres and I don't segment my audience. I've included both genres in my list ever since I started, and I can see no reason to separate them. Science Fiction and Fantasy are both speculative fiction. I read science fiction. I read fantasy, too. The two genres are enough alike that they will appeal to a broad range of the same people. What is more, across both genres, my style and voice and *brand* doesn't change.

My books tend to be realistic, gritty, and include political scheming. People who enjoy the Ambassador books might enjoy the Icefire books, too. They touch on a lot of similar themes even if one has magic and the other has space ships.

Don't assume that readers of one genre won't be interested in another fairly closely related genre. Assuming is self-rejection and the opposite of opportunity.

So I don't segment my list at the start, but instead I keep track of who clicks what. Remember advanced automation based on reader action? Well, this is where that comes in.

I group my readers according to the links they click.

The question is: once you've made these groups, what do you do with them?

Several things.

My newsletters are general. They include a bit of this and that about all of my series. I don't split them out according to genre or series.

But when I launch a new book, the segments become important. When you launch a book, you want most people arriving at your page on a retailer site to buy that book. You don't want them to leave without buying, or at least not at first. Retailer algorithms like it when a lot of people buy a book, so they are more likely to show the book to other people.

Working with your list's segments, a launch could look like this:

- Day 1: send to the list you gathered from sign-ups at the end of the previous book in the series
- Day 2: send to the people who have shown an interest in the series
- Day 3: send to the people interested in the book's genre, including the series in question
- Day 4: send to the rest of your list
- Day 5-10: ask your friends to send to their lists

A sequence like this will have the most powerful buyers first, and they will drive up the popularity of the book on retailer sites. If most people arriving at the page will buy the book, sites are more likely to show it to other people.

I also use the segmented groups to recruit people to send pre-release copies of later books in the series and to ask them questions about the series. This is especially useful if a series is ongoing.

So this is how I segregate my list without complete segmentation. It's based on what people click.

If, however, your genres are not terribly compatible, you may want two separate lists. For example, some of you received an email from me about the release of this book. That notice did not go to my fiction list or my competition list, except as a small one-line notice at the bottom.

To do list:

- Consider if you want to segregate your lists or keep them together.

THIRTY-TWO

About Open Rates And Click Rates

I OFTEN GET ASKED the question: what open rate should I aim for?

And I'm going to be honest with you. I'll tell you that I think it's the most stupid question you can ask yourself on the subject of mailing lists.

Why?

Because people's useless and stupid fixation with the open and click rate metrics distract them from the important stuff.

In the first place, let's do a little exercise.

Author A has a purely organic list with 500 people. He boasts that his open rate is 70%. That's 350 people.

Author B has a list of 10,000. She has just imported a big batch of competition entrants, and her open rate is lousy, 15%. That's 1500 people.

Now they both have a new release.

For author A, half the people who open the email buy the

book. That's actually too amazing to be true, but, let's just say, for argument's sake. That's 175 people.

For author B, only 11.7% of people who open the email will have to buy the book to achieve the same number of sales.

Depending on how attractive the book offer is, that may or may not happen. Author A is unlikely to get a quarter of his list to buy the book, either. There are many factors at play.

Again: now and forever into the future: it's always about the book. EVERYTHING comes back to whether people want to read the book. Do your utmost best to write a good book and make it look nice. Yes, I've said this before and will sound like a broken record (remember records?). It all begins and ends with the book. If the book doesn't work, then none of the rest of this will work either.

Right, and here is the magic of a front-end list:

Author B's large list is about *potential*. Author A has pretty much maxed out his audience. They may be wonderfully engaging, but there is next to zero growth potential in them unless he kills himself writing six books a year. Or unless a magical promotion suddenly brings in a huge influx of buyers who sign up for his list. But this relies on luck and stuff done by other people, and you may have noticed that I don't like to depend on this.

Imagine what happens if author B, through writing attractive emails with good titles, can lift her open rate to 20%. Imagine what she can do if she can write better emails to get a higher percentage of her list to buy her book.

There is also the fact that list B is unlikely to be static, because if author B has imported people from giveaways, she will likely do it again. So her open rate will be low, her unsubscribe rate high, but when she keeps adding people, the ones who open the emails and don't unsubscribe will eventually start to add up as a real audience. I will say a bit more about the list as moving target later.

Another exercise—if you ask 100 people: "If you're likely to get about 50 sales from either list A or list B, would you rather I sent it to list A of 100 people or list B of 1000 people?" I bet list B list wins every time. Because of the potential.

This is what front-end mailing lists are about: potential.

So what about the dude who boasted about his open rate of 70%? In the first place I want to say that he can run his list in whichever way he wants. But that high rate is a sure sign he's not using mailing lists to their potential. Most likely, he has already decided that this book is not for him. That's fine. If he's happy, that suits me.

But as any politician knows, you don't increase the number of people who vote for you by preaching to the choir. In order to increase your congregation, you have to step outside the church and talk to people in the street. This means you will not get wonderful engagement. Many people will ignore you. Some will even cross the road especially to avoid you. You are likely to occasionally piss people off. It's not about those people. It's about the people who are willing to go along with you and give you a chance to hear what you have to say.

In light of this, a high open rate means you're preaching to the choir. You're purely providing a back-end service, and if this is what you want, fine, but for crying out loud, don't boast about it as if it's somehow better than someone who is actively trying to increase their reach, OK?

On the flip side of the coin, a low open rate can mean a number of things:

- An unhealthy list, which may have been neglected

- A lot of non-organic sign-ups which still need sorting
- Obviously: room (and potential!) for improvement

Rather than staring yourself blind at the precise level of open and click rates (or even sillier: comparing them with other writers), study the steps you can take to increase them.

To do list:

- Keep an eye on your open and click rates.
- Take note of what increases them and what decreases them.

THIRTY-THREE

Cleaning Your List

IF YOU COLLECT MAILING list sign-ups from competitions or giveaways, your mailing list will grow very quickly.

It is natural that when people first join a list, they will open more emails than they will later on (see the honeymoon period).

This is part of a natural decay, and is normal.

However, if you import large numbers of email addresses, you will get some that the owners never check—because they use that address only to take part in giveaways—and your open rate will fall.

This matters because your provider rates all email list accounts. The deliverability of emails depends on this rating. Basically, your provider is interested in keeping their own rating high, so they will most likely favour email sent from accounts with the highest ratings.

For you, each extra subscriber is an added cost, so all of this is a roundabout way of saying that you may need to start thinking about culling some of these inactive people.

But who are they?

This is a very difficult subject, because the fact that your provider's statistics show that people are not opening your emails doesn't mean that this is actually true. There are situations when opens are not tracked, and people would show up as inactive when they have, in fact, opened every one of your emails.

You definitely wouldn't want to get rid of people like that.

I see authors send inactive people emails with the question if they still want to be on the list. The problem with those emails is that they annoy specifically the people we don't want to annoy: the ones who in fact open and read the emails, even if their opens are not registered.

It's a bit like something I'm sure we've all done: complained online about some habit, and the only people who felt that it was about them were the people who are your friends and acquaintances, and the people you were *really* talking about never even read the post. Long story short: don't annoy your regulars.

Then what to do, because you have a sizeable inactive group on your list. How to clean it up?

I advocate setting up some form of automation that cleans your list automatically as it grows. How you can do this will depend on your provider and what kind of tools they offer. They may offer an option in their automation sequence program to select readers who haven't opened certain emails. I don't know that any of them offer this as an automated process.

We will be using one metric that is a lot more reliable than opens: clicks. I have watched this across several mailings: the number of clicks reported in my MailerLite dashboard is virtually identical to the number reported on my website. Your provider knows the email addresses of the ones who click. You'll be using this.

The moment a subscriber enters my list, they go into two automations. One of them is the welcome sequence that I have described in basic automation, and the other only kicks into place about six months later. This automation sends them an email that says here is a free book. Now if they're on the ball and like free books, they will at least click the link. They may then realise that they already have the book. That doesn't matter because the email has fulfilled its purpose. I wanted them to open it. If they open and click, they're fine.

Then all the people who did not open that email will get a second email a month later with another free book and a differently worded title that does not include the word free. If they open that email, they get siphoned off back to the main group where they came from. So even if they already had that free book that also doesn't matter.

The group that matters is the ones who did not click either of those two emails. You can add more emails in the sequence if you want, or add one of these pinging emails every month and evaluate them after six months. It's up to you how you design it.

In any case, the people who have opened none of those emails are now sent a final email that asks them whether they still want to be on the list. At this point, when they get the email, the sequence has *already* unsubscribed them. The button goes to a resubscribe form.

Why is this better than the first option: sending all your inactive subscribers the same "do you still want to be on this list" email?

Because now you have filtered out your most active

subscribers, and you're not bugging them with needless stupid questions that will only annoy them. I bet that the remaining people are your most inactive ones. They may include a few who only seem inactive, because they read on their phones where their opens may not be registered; and maybe they'll be annoyed by the question. But most of those people will immediately click the button "Yes, please. I would like to keep getting your emails." And at least you've annoyed far fewer of them than if you'd sent "Do you still want to be on this list?" to start with. The rest—those who don't open and don't click that button— they're already gone.

Of course this is still an imprecise method, and the subject of list cleaning is not an easy one. False positives and false negatives are common. I've certainly been on a number of lists where I get auto-unsubscribed every so often.

In the end, as list owners, we have to strike a balance between trying to catch them all and trying to be a good citizen in the big bad eyes of the Internet. The Internet doesn't care about the people who open your emails but whose opens don't register. It rates you according to the ones that do. It's always a trade-off.

When you implement a cleaning process, you should keep a very close eye on your list metrics, because if they do not improve over a couple of mailings, then it's obviously not working and you should stop the process immediately.

Yes, there is a risk that you will automatically unsubscribe some people who were still interested.

It is quite unfortunate, but needs to be weighed up against the cost of carrying a lot of subscribers who don't open at all. If people complain to you, it might be wise to ask them to use a different email address, since this often solves the problem.

Also remember that the honeymoon period also applies to

subscribers individually. They are most likely to read and open your emails after they have just joined. After a while, they might find the next shiny thing and the next favourite email list, and will not open your emails as often any more. You might even get them to open again if they go through a resubscribe process. But even if people still say they want to be on your list, they may not read your emails. And meanwhile you're paying for them so maybe you are better off not having them. These are all things you can think about, and decisions you must make for yourself.

To do list:

- Consider methods to clean your list of non-openers.
- If you want to implement an automation sequence for this, it needs to be put in place when people join your list.

THIRTY-FOUR

The List As Moving Target

I THINK FAR TOO MANY authors see their list and audience as a static audience.

While it is true that some groups, like diehard fans, will be a lot more static than, say, people who signed up to get a freebie, the truth is that *both* groups move. New people sign up and, sad as it may be, people leave, even on a purely organic list comprised of back-of-book sign-ups. People simplify their lives, people are too far behind with their reading, people didn't enjoy your new series because it's outside what they usually read, people move on, and yes, they die, too.

It's an email marketing ballpark standard assumption that the natural decay of your list will be 20% per year. That's quite a lot, and will obviously vary per list, but don't ever make the mistake of treating your list as a static entity. It's a constantly moving amoeba that not only gets shaped by your effort, but by the members of the list themselves, as they reply and ask you for certain things.

Moving and evolving is a good thing.

Why do you think websites of major companies change all the

time, and every business does an overhaul of their presentation to customers every so often?

New things, and a change in presentation, attract new people. If you stop attracting new people, you start moving backwards, because people continuously leave at the other end. It's their right to do this, and you can't stop it. You have to attract new readers who are still in that stage that they will blurt to everyone who wants to hear it that they've discovered this great new author. The honeymoon period. It wears off for any relationship, personal, commercial or based on knowledge and learning. People have heard it all and they move on.

Plan for it.

To do list:

- Always be prepared to revamp your list, to redesign emails and landing pages, to start new lists and retire old ones (and ask people to follow you to the new list)

THIRTY-FIVE

Rules About Mailing Lists

SO HERE ARE THE important take-aways about mailing lists:

Natural decay

People will leave, all the time. This may hurt, but it's mostly not about you.

Treat your list as a market stall where you're trying to engage people so that they will buy your apples. Some people will have no time and will move along even if you give them a free piece. Some will just want to chat, but have no money, and some decide that they'd rather have oranges. This is normal. Your list is *not for those people*, and you want to remove as many of them as you can. It's about the people who stay, the people who like apples.

In order to engage them, you must tell them about your apples, and give them free samples so that if they can at all be motivated to buy apples, they know that yours are great.

But you will fail with the majority of people. It's about the ones who stay.

Never assume

Assuming is the enemy of mailing list operation. Never assume what they want, ask them questions instead.

Don't assume that they don't want to be bothered. If they really didn't, they wouldn't have given you their email address. And those people who wanted only new release notifications would have signed up for this service at Amazon or Bookbub. These people want to hear from you, because they think authors are cool.

Don't assume that they have read all your books, even the ones who signed up to your back-end list.

Never assume that they are of a certain age, a certain gender or live in certain countries. Ask them. The results will probably surprise you.

To do list:

- Regularly survey your list (use Google Forms, it's free).
- Keep it anonymous.
- Ask them which books they've read.
- Ask them where they live, their age, their interests, the genres they read.
- Make decisions based on your answers.

THIRTY-SIX

Of Mailing Lists And Money

HOW MUCH IS a mailing list worth? And how much should you spend on acquiring subscribers?

There are as many different answers to this question as there are writers. Some writers go into extremely detailed calculations. The problem is that although numbers, percentages and dollars and cents may look impressive, the resulting values are not worth much if the underlying assumptions are unsound.

You can ask how many books people on your list have bought, but because a survey is self-selective, people who have not bought any of your books won't fill it out. This will make your estimate too high. Also, investigating your current lists doesn't take into consideration all those people who you paid to acquire but who have since unsubscribed.

For this reason, I use a whole-list calculation for the value of my list.

I consider income from the list:

- How many books do you typically sell off the back of a new release?

- How many people then typically buy other books? (Sell-through percentage, which you can estimate from retailer figures)
- How many new books do you release per year?
- Affiliate income

And expenses of the list:

- Cost of running your list
- Cost of acquiring new subscribers, if they're Facebook ads, buy-in amounts for giveaways or cross-promotion services etc.

Calculate incoming and outgoing over a year to see if your list is costing you money or making money. If your list is new, I wouldn't sweat costs too much, but once you have a decent catalogue of books and your list is costing you money, then there is obviously something wrong. It could be a matter of time, but ultimately, you want your list to generate more income from a new release than if you got a Bookbub ad.

There are a number of ways to increase income from your list:

- Apply strategies to make more people open your emails and click links and buy books. Read some email marketing books.
- Release more books in series that people on your list want to buy
- Increase the price of backlist books
- Reduce the cost of running the list by cleaning it or using a different provider
- Increase affiliate income

Increasing your subscribers can be a double-edged sword, because they will typically cost you more and this cost is not always immediately set off by a corresponding increase in sales.

To do list:

- Tally income and expenditure from your list on a regular basis to gauge the health of your strategy.
- Make changes if you're not happy.

THIRTY-SEVEN

Spam Is Meat That Comes In A Can

SPAM REPORTS, the bane of anyone with a mailing list.

They're pretty much inevitable. The occasional person will sign up, download your freebies and then report you for spam.

I know, I know, these people shouldn't be allowed to exist.

But they do.

Often people don't realise that a spam report can be generated by something that seems as harmless as moving an email to the junk folder.

But all of a sudden you happen to send an email that has a disproportionate number of spam reports and you're in trouble with your list provider.

This is especially a problem when your list is small. You compound the problem by not emailing your list frequently.

Why?

Well, as I said before, it's all about *percentages*.

If you email 100 people and two report you for spam (read:

innocuously move your email to the junk folder), you have a problem. Email to 1000 people and those two don't present a problem at all. Even four people wouldn't be a problem.

Leave 3 months between one email and the next, and 50% of those 100 people have forgotten who you are. Many of them will go "who the hell is this?" and move your email into the junk folder. Bingo. Another spam report.

If you have only 500 people on your list in total, then this is a huge percentage.

So, to avoid spam reports, absolutely do these things:

- Import big lists in batches. Better still, if you're doing giveaways, use an automatic cross-promotion sign-up service like Bookfunnel, which trickles subscribers into your list.
- Don't leave it too long between emails.
- Use clear subject lines.
- In the first email, remind people why they signed up.
- Make it super-easy for them to unsubscribe. Put the unsubscribe button at the top of the first email. Frustrated people will make deliberate spam reports. If people don't want to be there, you really don't want them on your list either.
- A lesser-known option to significantly cut the number of spam reports is to use your own unsubscribe page. MailChimp gives you the option to redirect people to your own page once they hit "unsubscribe", bypassing their standard "why did you unsubscribe" questionnaire. One of the options in that questionnaire is "I never signed up", but if you've been diligent in collecting emails, this is patently untrue, and if they choose this option—because they

can't remember that they signed up—it will result in a spam report.

MailerLite does not offer this option, but it does offer the option to automatically unsubscribe someone who clicks a link. Make a button at the bottom of the email that says "unsubscribe", make the link go to a page on your website that says "You are now unsubscribed" and unsubscribe them automatically as soon as they do this.

To do list:

- Make sure it's easy for people to find the unsubscribe option.
- If you can, direct people to a page on your own site rather than the provider-supplied "why did you unsubscribe" page.

THIRTY-EIGHT

Too Much Email

EVERY NOW AND THEN, people will complain that email marketing will fall down in a heap because "people get too much email".

There is no such thing as too much email. These days email is sent when parcels ship, when they're delivered, when there are statements in your bank account, when something you ordered is available.

Too much?

You *asked* for those emails. They deliver information you want.

There is only such thing as email that people don't find interesting enough to keep receiving. And the funny thing about this type of email is: people self-select.

So while it is wholly possible that an individual went on a downloading spree from authors who gave out free books in return for their email address, and this person is now dismayed at the quantity of email hitting their inbox, this is a receiver problem, and not a sender-induced problem.

But everyone is signing up for author newsletters!

Yes, they are. Chances are that any time in the past ten years, when you have bought something online, you've also been signed up to almost all of those sites' newsletters. Online stores have used email marketing since the beginning of email marketing. Authors are just catching up. If email marketing didn't work, why do you think major stores (like Amazon) would do it? They wouldn't.

But everyone is getting so many author newsletters!

Maybe, but as the discoverability of good books on Amazon has declined markedly, there are other ways readers find out about books, and author newsletters are high on the list.

Make no mistake, people who don't want to be on your list will take themselves off. That's what you want them to do from the moment they join: if they don't read your books, you want them to unsubscribe.

"Too much email" is about the receiver, not about the sender. The receiver can decide to simplify their inbox and get rid of newsletters they either don't need anymore or are no longer interested in. Especially the first type is something you don't hear mentioned a lot. If a newsletter is an automated learning program about a service, and I've been through it, I don't need the emails anymore. Does that also mean that I won't use the site anymore? That's a different thing. Email marketing automation sequences *teach* people things. When they've been taught what the company wants them to know, they can leave.

Which brings me to . . .

THIRTY-NINE

But I Don't Want To Annoy People!

OK, SUPPOSING YOU sent a mailing to 1000 people, and 30% opened the email. You also received two replies: one with a positive comment about the email you sent, the other complaining: "All authors are sending me email these days!"

Which do you think will bother you more: the fact that 299 people read the email and one even bothered to send you a nice reply, or the fact that one person (who, my guess is, probably complains about everything in life) complained to you?

I bet it's the last one.

It's ridiculous, isn't it?

Almost THREE HUNDRED people read your email, and you're going to worry about ONE email from someone who doesn't appear to have noticed that the email comes with an unsubscribe button. Wait, why don't you just engage it on her behalf? You don't need people like that on your list.

You should care about delivering value to those 299 people, because *they* are your audience.

This is why I said, at the beginning of the book, to lock up your sense of wanting to be liked by everyone, because it's impossible. When you start running a sizeable email list, you will find that there is no end to the supply of weird, rude and stupid people in the world. There are also many really nice ones, but strangely enough those don't tend to get under our skin so much.

A mailing list is about your mandate, sticking to it and pleasing the majority of your subscribers—most of whom will only complain if a download link doesn't work. And oh, then you will find out how many people really appreciate what you're doing.

Those people, that silent majority, are your people. Your audience. Your crew. They may not always be very vocal, but they're there.

FORTY

Help, I'm F(l)ailing

HANG ON A MOMENT, I hear people say. I did everything you told me to do. I set up a website, started a mailing list, did some cross-promotions and I now have 4000 people on my list. There is only one problem: they don't buy my books! They're just costing me money.

I'm going to be asking you some questions:

Q: How long have they been on your list?

A: Two months.

Q: How many emails have you sent them?

A: Two, and each time I send them something, about a hundred unsubscribe! It's terrible. This list is useless.

Now hang on a moment. You make the judgement after two emails and two whole months? You don't recognise that unsubscribes are, in fact, a good thing in this case?

You have barely given people the chance to read your free book. Do you think it was the only free book they've ever downloaded?

The most important ingredient here is time. To turn a front-end subscriber from a giveaway into a reader takes time and effort. You have to send them interesting stuff. Talk about interesting research you did for your book. Show pictures of the locality. Talk about things relating to your book. Recipes, facts about medieval clothing, spaceship designs. Tell them anecdotes about writing. Tell them what you do each day, how you got into writing, why you chose your cover artist. Anything, in fact, that is interesting but didn't get included in your books.

Give them little things, like free short stories; tell them about your friends' books, let them know when one of your books is on special.

Do this on a regular basis. I would not leave much more than two weeks between emails. Don't give them the chance to forget who you are.

Most importantly: keep doing this. Also keep evaluating your results. Compare open rates between different types of subject lines. In general: more direct works much better than clever. People have no time for clever. If they don't get it because they're not in the right mind frame to think about it, they'll delete your email. Bam. There's another spam report.

FORTY-ONE

Patience Really Is A Virtue

THE MAILING LIST strategy does not come on its own. There is not much point in developing a large list if you have nothing to sell them. I see people acquiring huge mailing list, but all they have is one or two books and no complete series, or a couple of short novellas that they sell for $.99. It's virtually impossible to recoup your mailing list cost from that.

So the first thing you must always do is to keep writing. Because there is no point to doing any of this if you don't write. You must keep adding to your intellectual property, preferably in ways in which your readers like to consume it. Also think about different formats, and uploading to different sites. You must give your audience as much chance to buy your work as possible. And then you must keep them happy.

Writing new work is always the core of your business. Whether you write fast or slowly, as long as readers see that new material is forthcoming, they are happy to hang around and wait for it.

The mailing list is especially important if you don't write terribly fast. Because if you release nothing new for a couple of months, the algorithms on the retailer websites will have forgotten about you. Your books will no longer be recommended to other readers, because there are newer books available for people to buy. It is in the retailers' interest to always have the latest best-selling books on the front page. By using your mailing list you can redirect the focus to your books.

Building up a sizeable catalogue of books which you can sell to new subscribers takes a fair bit of time. This is the basis of the three-year plan. If you write four books a year, and you do this for three years, you will have twelve books. This is a decent catalogue that you can play with. If you have much less than that, everything becomes harder. It's harder to make advertising work for you, it's harder to make a mailing list work for you. It's harder to get reviews, and harder to get and keep readers. So if you're at that stage, the best thing you can do is to double down and finish more books, finish series that you started, start new ones and simply put out more product for your readers to buy.

A recent survey done by the owners of Freebooksy showed that authors who earn six figures or more per year have an average of thirty books in their catalogue. A lot of them have no bestsellers, and most of them are not well-known names. They are what the publishing industry used to call midlist authors. It is well known that the publishing industry has been squeezing these authors out. As the size of industry advances has declined, it has become harder for those authors to make a living. Many of them have moved to self-publishing, and have taken their sizeable catalogue with them.

Another category of writers able to splash onto the scene quite quickly includes the writers who never sold a novel, but spent years querying agents and publishers. They might have gotten close to a deal, but never actually signed one. Meanwhile, they had lots of books sitting on their computers. When self-publishing came along, all they needed to do was pull out these old manuscripts, give them a light re-edit, send them off to an editor and a cover designer, and publish them. It might have looked like they were brand new, but they had been writing and honing their craft for years.

The main indicator for earnings of authors is the amount of content they sell. There are some authors who are lucky and hit with one book, but that is extremely rare, and has always been so. The power is in backlist. So you have to make sure that you have backlist. Yes, it's hard. This is not an industry for wimps and chickens. But you knew that already didn't you?

The same survey also showed that almost all of those authors pay for editing, and cover design, and that many of them employed people to do other tasks. I mention this here to illustrate that these people are committed to putting out the best product they can. As a new author, this is the part of their business plan you should emulate. Write a lot of good books, make sure they're connected, either because of your name or because they are series, package them well, and feed them into your catalogue.

Once these books are there, you can start doing interesting things with them. Use the first books as free content to give away in return for mailing addresses, use the first books in ads, do cross-promotions using those first books. But none of it works without the subsequent books to sell, where you make your money. So you must be patient and set this system up first. Write the books, publish some, start a list, increase your list, start automation, publish more books, then encourage new subscribers to buy from your backlist.

This is the basis of the three-year plan. Now get beavering!

About the Author

Patty Jansen lives in Sydney, Australia, where she spends most of her time writing Science Fiction and Fantasy.

Her story *This Peaceful State of War* placed first in the second quarter of the Writers of the Future contest and was published in their 27th anthology. She has also sold fiction to genre magazines such as Analog Science Fiction and Fact, Redstone SF and Aurealis.

Patty has written over twenty novels in both Science Fiction and Fantasy, including the *Icefire Trilogy* and the *Ambassador* series.

pattyjansen.com

Books by Patty Jansen

MORE INFORMATION:
PATTYJANSEN.COM

Notes

1. This Is A Book About Email Marketing For Authors

1. Except Bookbub. You should never stop applying for Bookbub.

5. The Trifecta Of Mailing List Rules

1. You know I'm joking about the neon colours, right?

21. The Ultimate Function Of Your List

1. Never use affiliate codes in an email. Not only do certain affiliate providers dislike this, but it reduces click rates. Make a page on your website and include the affiliate links there. As a bonus, you can include all links for all retailers on the same page.

www.ingramcontent.com/pod-product-compliance
Lightning Source LLC
Chambersburg PA
CBHW071502080526
44587CB00014B/2188